Sixty-Six
First Dates

He is faithful!
Lam. 3:22-23
Gretchyn Quernemoen

Sixty-Six
First Dates

Every Day Offers a New Chance
to Fall in Love with God

Gretchyn Quernemoen

REDEMPTION
PRESS

Published by Redemption Press, PO Box 427, Enumclaw, WA 98022.

This book is printed on acid-free paper.

Printed in the United States of America

ISBN 13: 978-1-63232-958-5

Library of Congress Control Number: 2014907294

Contents

Week 8

Week 9

Week 10

Acknowledgments

I owe a debt of gratitude to Kristin Salvevold, Deb Brown, Sue Williams, and Barb Fluth for helping me edit this book. I could not have finished it without their advice and wisdom. They sacrificed their time and used their talents to help me, and in doing so, they encouraged me to follow God's plan for this book.

The two little words *thank you* don't even come close to expressing how grateful I am to everyone who's prayed for this book. They know who they are! I hit a standstill many times and knew I couldn't continue without their prayers. Every time I reached out to ask for prayer, they were faithful, and God gave me exactly what I needed to keep going. They prayed for my decision to publish a blog, they prayed for a publisher, they prayed for me to keep on schedule, and they prayed for marketing information when I had no clue how to proceed. Without them and their faithful prayers, this book would not exist.

I thank my husband, Barry, and our kids, Caleb and Shalyn, who have supported me throughout this process. They believed in me, encouraged me, and prayed for me daily. They gave me time alone when I needed to write. They even inspired some of the devotions and gave me something to write about! Barry's support for me in this process has been one of the biggest blessings in my life. I thank him for letting me pursue my dream and for encouraging me every step of the way! I love him and our kids so much!

I offer special thanks to Wayne and Joy Wensmann, two very dear friends and fellow believers in Christ. Although Wayne is now in heaven, his encouragement of my writing will always stick with me. He was one of the few men brave enough to read my blog gqtoo.blogspot.com. If there were ever a few days or weeks when I didn't post on my blog, I would get a text from Wayne asking, "GQToo, where are you?" Those few words always provided inspiration to get me writing again. Joy has been a wonderful blessing as a prayer warrior for this book. She was the first to place an order for ten copies, showing her faith in me and in the message of this book.

There are too many other special people to mention, so I will conclude by saying a huge thanks to all of my friends and my family. I could not have done this without them, and I feel extremely blessed that they are part of my life. May God bless their faithfulness!

With love and a full heart,
Gretchyn

Why Sixty-Six?

You may be wondering why I have used the number sixty-six in the title of this book. It is a strange number, I admit. The answer has to do with habits. You may be familiar with the theory that a habit is formed in twenty-one days, because that's the number so often cited in the media. A cosmetic surgeon came up with the idea in the 1960s, and the claim was repeated so many times that it eventually became accepted as fact.

Current research has found that sixty-six days are usually required to form a habit. Research shows that if you can do something for sixty-six days straight, you will most likely be able to do it for a year, for five years, or for the rest of your life. Sixty-six is not a magic number, though, because some people need less time to establish a habit and others need more. My hope is that after sixty-six first dates with God, spending daily time with Him will become a habit you'll never want to break!

Introduction

Who can forget the excitement and the anticipation of a first date? I remember my first date with my husband as if it happened yesterday. He had asked me to play tennis because he knew it was my favorite sport. The date started off well as we warmed up and chatted at the same time. We played a few games, and then it was time to switch sides on the court. As I walked around the net, he ran straight toward the middle of it and glided over it. Was I ever amazed and impressed by that smooth move!

I also had some first dates that didn't go so well. There were times when I knew that the first date would also be the last date. It's disappointing to go on a first date and realize that it's not working for one or both of you. I don't ever want to relive those painful evenings of small talk or, worse yet, awkward silence.

When I was in my midthirties, I found myself desperately needing a first date of a different kind—a first date with God. I had grown up in a Christian home and had attended church faithfully twice a week. I had graduated from a Christian college and had married a Christian man. How was it, then, that I found myself still struggling in my relationship with God? One reason was that I had a lot of head knowledge, but that knowledge didn't always reach my heart.

Then something happened that revolutionized my relationship with God. A friend gave me *The One Year Chronological Bible*. This Bible fluently spoke the language of my logical brain! As I read about the events of the Bible in the order they occurred, I started to see God for who He is, not for who I thought He should be.

I saw a God of justice. I read about the devastation of the flood and grappled with the reality that the God I serve wiped out the human race (except for Noah's family, of course!). I saw a God of mercy as over and over again I read about how the Lord took care of His people, the Israelites, despite their disrespectful and untrusting hearts. I saw myself in the Israelites of the Old Testament as well as in the crowd that called for Jesus' crucifixion in the New Testament.

I can honestly say that every time I opened that Bible and asked God to show me something about Himself, He did. Plain and simple. It wasn't always what I wanted to see or what I'd remembered from childhood Bible stories, but it was always the truth about God.

After a year, I found myself only about one-third of the way through this Bible. Since I am a bit of a rule follower, it really bothered me that I hadn't finished in the allotted time! However, God showed me that I needed to give myself grace. He made it clear to me that it wasn't how quickly I read through the Bible that mattered, but that I was reading His Word on a daily basis. I began blogging about the insights I was finding in Scripture each day. My life was changing drastically through my daily dates with God, and I wanted others to have the same experience.

For my fortieth birthday, a friend printed out a hard copy of every blog entry I'd written. Seeing my thoughts in print inspired me to ask some friends to pray with me for one month about the future of those entries. I thank God for the faithful friends who believed in me, encouraged me, and prayed me through that time! At the end of the month, I could feel God's Spirit nudging me to publish the blog.

The day after I felt this prompting, I sent out another request for prayer, because I had no idea where to begin with the publishing process. The next morning, I received an e-mail from a friend with a link about self-publishing. With each passing day, it became clearer that God was opening the doors for me to publish this devotional book, and I knew I needed to be brave and to walk through them.

I quickly realized that publishing a book would take much more determination and hard work than I'd ever imagined. I will never pick up a book again without appreciating the time and effort that go into writing, editing, designing, and publishing a manuscript. There were many days throughout this process when I felt inadequate and questioned my abilities. However, *Sixty-Six First Dates* is a testimony to God's faithfulness and is proof that He answers prayer.

I hope you enjoy the journey of falling in love with God as much as I have—and still do! I wish I could meet each individual who reads this book. I would love to hear your story. Maybe you've never picked up a Bible before. Maybe you don't even know if you believe in God. Maybe you know the Lord, but you've gotten out of the habit of spending time with Him. Maybe you just wanted a new devotional book, and so here you are.

No matter where you're at in your spiritual journey, I pray that God's Word will penetrate your heart in a new and fresh way. May God richly bless the time you spend in His presence, and may you revel in every first date with Him!

Suggestions for How to Use This Book

As a personal devotional

This book is designed to be read every day for sixty-six days straight. It is intended to help you make a habit out of spending time in God's Word and in prayer. However, if you miss a day, please don't give up! Give yourself grace and start again the next day.

Start with prayer. Over the years I have learned that God speaks to us when our hearts are open to hear His truth. I've made a habit of praying a simple, yet heartfelt prayer to prepare to read from God's Word. I suggest this prayer based on Psalm 119:18: *Open my eyes to see the wonderful truths in Your instructions, and please show me any sin in my life that would hinder this precious time with You.*

Read the assigned Scripture for the day. Feel free to use the Bible translation of your choice. You may use the notes/prayer section provided in the book to write down your observations about each passage.

Make the scripted prayer your conversation with God. Then add your prayer requests and praises in the notes/prayer section. These requests will be a great encouragement later when you see how God has answered them.

Respond to the call to action. Use the notes/prayer segment to record your response.

For use with small groups

Over a cup of coffee or tea, take time each week or two to get together with a group and discuss what you're learning. Here are some suggestions for what you might do.

- Read the Scripture passages together.
- Share your answers to the calls to action.
- Hold each other accountable for spending time with God each day.
- Pray for each other. Share your requests and praises with the group so that you can all enjoy the blessing of watching God respond.

You will seek me and find me when you
seek me with all of your heart.
—Jeremiah 29:13

Week 1

Date 1: Later Is Now

Scripture Reading: Psalm 63

It was a beautiful summer day. It was so nice out, in fact, that I decided I would start the day by going for a walk. After all, if I waited until later to exercise, it would never happen. As I tied my tennis shoes, my thoughts drifted to the Bible on my coffee table. I paused at the door and briefly considered doing my devotions, but I decided I could do them when I got back.

After my walk, I decided I should shower. Then I needed to get the kids some breakfast and start a load of laundry. I had been wanting to teach the kids to play tennis, and this was perfect tennis weather. I told them to grab their rackets, and we headed off to the courts. When we got home, it was time to make lunch. I switched the load of clothes, and my thoughts drifted back to the Bible on the table. *Later, after lunch,* I thought.

After lunch, some neighbor kids rang our doorbell and asked my kids to play outside. Since the kids seemed entertained, I decided to stain another section of our deck. Before long, it was time to think about supper. I came inside and walked right past my Bible, putting off my devotions until bedtime.

Supper came and went, and afterward our family completed some chores and then it was bed time. By then, I was too tired to do my devotions. I rationalized that I would get up early the next day and spend time with God.

Even though the day had been great, I felt empty inside. Something was missing. We enjoyed a fun and fairly productive day, yet it did not feel complete. Deep down I knew what was missing. I said a quick prayer before bed, promising myself I'd spend the first part of the next day with God.

Later.

The next morning I walked downstairs and saw my Bible. I realized what time it was.

It was later.

Sitting down on my favorite chair, I started reading my Bible. I felt God speaking to me through His Word, soothing and comforting me. I felt centered and loved. The sad thing is that He wanted me to feel these things the day before, but I had ignored Him. He could have encouraged me and strengthened me, but I kept telling Him, "Later."

No matter what time of day it is, if you haven't spent time with God yet, later is now!

Prayer: *Lord, I'm sorry for passing You by. I'm sorry for walking past my Bible when I should be stopping to spend time with You. I'm sorry that I've made other things in my life more important than my relationship with You. Please forgive me and meet me today through Your Word. Amen.*

Do you find yourself putting time with God on a back shelf? What can you do to change later to now?

Notes/Prayer Requests & Praises

Prayer Request - Please help me to forgive myself of my mistakes and others. and not to be judgemental on myself for forgetting things

Date 2: Wake Up Tomorrow

Scripture Reading: Lamentations 3:21-26

One day when my daughter was in third grade, she came home from school crying. Her bad day got even worse when she made poor choices at home and I sent her to her room without an after-school snack. I told her she could come out of her room when she was ready to have a good attitude. When she didn't come out for quite a while, I decided to check on her.

Opening her bedroom door, I saw that her room was black. My eyes searched for her in the darkness, and I finally found her lying in her bed under the covers. I slowly crawled under the blankets with her and asked what was wrong. She replied, "I just want to go to sleep and wake up tomorrow when it's a new day."

Amen, sister!

I can relate; can you? I've had days when all I wanted to do was lie in bed under the covers, fall asleep, and wake up the next day.

Maybe Jeremiah felt the same way. In Lamentations, he says that every day can have a new beginning, which makes me think he also had days when he wanted to crawl under the covers and hide out until morning!

He says, "Yet this I call to mind and therefore I have hope: Because of the Lord's great love we are not consumed, for His compassions never fail. They are *new every morning;* great is Your faithfulness" (Lamentations 3:21-23, emphasis mine).

Amen, brother!

Prayer: *Lord, thank You that my hope is in You and not in the things of this world. Your compassions are new every morning. Great is Your faithfulness! Amen.*

Read Lamentations 3:21-23 out loud five to ten times. Speaking the verses will help to brand them on your heart and give them power in your life. Each time you speak these verses, emphasize different words and phrases, and they will give you a vision of God's love, compassion, and hope.

Notes/Prayer Requests & Praises

_____

_____

_____

_____

_____

_____

_____

_____

_____

_____

_____

_____

_____

Date 3: Beyond Romance

Scripture Reading: Jeremiah 31:1-14

I find a good love story irresistible. I can't pass up a romantic movie or book with its incomparable mix of laughter, joy, heartache, and of course, love. If you enjoy a good romance as much as I do, grab a cup of coffee or tea and keep reading. You're in for a treat!

The story I'm going to tell began in the 1940s, a time when young men from across the nation left the comforts of home to serve in World War II. The prospect of leaving for war must have been terrifying, but a young man named Ken Jensen found comfort in receiving letters from his hometown in western Minnesota. The letters from a young lady named Lillian were especially sweet!

As Ken's and Lil's letters traveled back and forth across the miles, an intimate friendship began. That friendship grew into love, and Ken and Lil were married on July 19, 1946. Their love story continued as they raised five children. Life wasn't always easy, but their commitment to each other and their love for God helped them navigate the joys and the trials of life.

During a typical wedding ceremony, most people repeat the vows, "For better or for worse, in sickness and in health, until death do us part." Most of us cannot imagine the "worse" part or the "sickness" part unless it becomes a reality. Ken and Lil experienced both health and sickness. However, with God's strength, even the adversity of illness could not diminish their love.

Lil suffered from memory loss during the later years of her life. Sometimes she would remember her children and Ken when they came to visit, but eventually her memory slipped further and further away. However, not even Lil's fading memory could weaken Ken's love for her. In the three years that Lil was in a memory care center, Ken visited her faithfully every day except three, when he was too sick to leave the house.

Ken loved Lil with his whole heart until the day she died at age eighty-six. I had the privilege of witnessing this love story since Ken and Lil are my grandpa and my grandma. As I watched my grandpa lovingly care for his wife of sixty-five years until the day she met Jesus, a thought entered my mind: *Oh, to be loved like that.*

My next thought was, *I am loved like that!* In Jeremiah 31:3, the Lord says, "I have loved you with an everlasting love; I have drawn you with loving-kindness." The Lord shows us His devotion in a love story for the ages! I witnessed a beautiful example of affection between my grandpa and my grandma, but my heavenly Father loves me even more than my earthly mind can imagine.

Prayer: *Heavenly Father, thank You for loving me with an everlasting love. Thank You for showing me what true love is by sending Your Son Jesus to earth as a sacrifice for my sins. Thank You for giving me my very own love story. Amen.*

Write out Jeremiah 31:3 and stick it in your coat pocket or somewhere close to you so that you will feel the love from this verse.

Notes/Prayer Requests & Praises

_____

_____

_____

_____

_____

_____

Date 4: Control Freak

Scripture Reading: James 4:13-15

I've been called a lot of things including *type A, a leader,* and *organized.* You get the picture! One thing I've never been called is *flexible.* There's a good reason for that: I'm not flexible. I don't like anything to change my plans or to get in the way of what's been scheduled. Right now you're probably thinking one of two things: *I can relate* or *Why doesn't she chill out?*

If you're thinking I should chill out, you're right! Always being in control hasn't brought me the happiness and the fulfillment I thought it would. Somehow I thought that by controlling all aspects of my life, I could insulate myself from the disappointments and the challenges that life could bring. However, I am realizing that by trying to run my life, I am missing out on living life to the fullest.

Whenever I struggle with the area of control, the Lord points me to James 4:13-15, which says, "Now listen, you who say, 'Today or tomorrow we will go to this city or that city, spend a year there, carry on business and make money.' Why, you don't even know what will happen tomorrow. What is your life? You are a mist that appears for a little while and then vanishes. Instead, you ought to say, 'If it is the Lord's will, we will live and do this or that.'"

If that's not convicting for a chronic controller, I don't know what is! Basically, these verses are saying, "Who do you think you are? Are you so presumptuous that you think you have any control over your life?"

The idea is silly and even laughable when you think about it. To think that any of us has control over our lives or those of family members is crazy. These verses are a wake-up call to a control freak like me. No wonder God wants me to read them over and over again!

Now comes the interesting part. What does it mean to give up the control that I so dearly love? I know God will reveal the answer to me as I seek His will for my life. Hey, maybe I can give up control in small pieces. That would be nice, but I know I'm missing the point. This control freak has a lot to learn!

Prayer: *Lord, I am sorry for thinking that I can control anything in my life. By not being open to Your plan, I know I have been missing out on blessings that You would have loved to give me. I want to let You be in charge of my life and to follow Your will. Amen.*

What part of your life does God want control over?

Notes/Prayer Requests & Praises

_____

_____

_____

_____

_____

_____

_____

_____

_____

_____

Date 5: I Don't Do Mornings

Scripture Readings: Genesis 4:1-12; Leviticus 23:9-14

If you know me, then you know I am not a morning person. I don't like to talk to people (including my poor husband) and I'm definitely not friendly or pleasant at that time of the day. One of my friends will ask me if I've had a cup of coffee before attempting to approach me! Knowing this about me will make what I'm going to say all the more ironic.

During a weekly women's Bible study, I felt convicted to spend more time alone with God. I realized that if I wanted to hear from Him, I needed to spend more time in His Word and in prayer.

As I was thinking about this, the term *firstfruits* popped into my head. It's a strange word, and I wondered why it came to mind. I knew I'd heard it in the Bible, so I did some research. I found the word in Leviticus 23:9-14, which mentions the Feast of Firstfruits. This feast required that the first crops harvested be offered to God. The Israelites could not eat the food from their harvest until they had made this offering.

I felt like God was speaking to me through this passage, telling me to give the firstfruits of my time to Him. For some reason, I felt like He wanted my mornings. The thought made me chuckle because God knows everything about me. He knows what I'm like in the morning, and I couldn't believe He wanted to spend the first part of the day with me. However, if anyone can handle me in the morning, it's God. Actually, He's probably the only one who can handle me in the morning!

I decided to start spending the first ten minutes of each morning with God. It may not seem like a lot, but for a nonmorning person, it was a start!

Maybe mornings don't work for you. Maybe afternoons or evenings work better. The important thing is that you spend quality time with God each day. It doesn't have to be a huge quantity of time, because that can seem overwhelming at first. Offering the firstfruits of your time means giving uninterrupted, dedicated time to God. Time to read His Word, to pray, and to listen to His voice.

God wants our best—whether that means time, finances, or anything else He asks of us. And He deserves it! Whether you're a night person like me or a morning person (I know you're out there), you'll discover what God has in store for you when you give Him the best of your time.

Prayer: *Lord, Scripture says that You want the first and the best from all I do. You want me to spend time alone with You each day. Thank You for desiring to spend time with me. It's an unbelievable privilege to spend time with the Creator of the universe. From now on I will set aside time each day to devote to You. Amen.*

Specify right now at what time you will commune with God each day. Give yourself grace to adjust that time as the week continues. The most important thing is not when you spend time with God but that you are doing it each day.

Notes/Prayer Requests & Praises

_____

_____

_____

_____

_____

_____

Date 6: Fifty First Dates

Scripture Reading: Psalm 12

As I said in yesterday's devotion, I'm not a morning person. I remember two mornings when I was particularly out of it. After I woke up on the first day, I read a psalm, then prayed. The next day I read the same psalm by accident. I didn't even remember that I'd read it the day before. The first day I hadn't underlined or highlighted anything, but the second day the words of that psalm jumped off the pages of my Bible and spoke to my heart.

At first I felt a little embarrassed at my mistake. How could I have read a psalm the previous morning and not remembered it? Not only that, but how could I have gotten so much out of the psalm on day two when the previous day I hadn't highlighted anything?

This scenario reminded me of the movie *50 First Dates*, starring Adam Sandler and Drew Barrymore. While I am by no means endorsing this movie, the story has some value. Barrymore's character has amnesia and never remembers the previous day. Sandler's character spends every day wooing her until she falls in love with him. Then he wakes up the next morning and starts from square one. He loves her so much that he is willing to spend fifty first dates with her.

Drew Barrymore's character begins each day with a fresh perspective on life. (Wouldn't it be nice sometimes not to remember what happened yesterday?) In real life, we can gain a positive outlook on each day by spending time with God. We can have fifty-plus first dates with Him.

It doesn't matter if we get up and read the same Scripture verses again, because sometimes a passage will affect us differently than it did the last time we read it. The important thing is that we spend time in God's Word each day. We shouldn't get frustrated if we don't remember everything we've read, because maybe what we read was just enough to get us through that day.

Prayer: *Heavenly Father, thank You for the Bible and the new insight I can receive each time I read it. Thank You that while Your Word is the same yesterday, today, and tomorrow, You can use it to show me something fresh every day. Thank You for the life-giving resource I have in the Bible. Amen.*

After reading Psalm 12, what new perspective or insight did you gain? If you have trouble thinking of something, read this passage again and ask God what He wants to show you.

Notes/Prayer Requests & Praises

_____

_____

_____

_____

_____

_____

_____

_____

_____

_____

_____

Date 7: Shut Up and Listen

Scripture Reading: Psalm 46

Being still is a foreign concept to me. Sometimes when I pray or read my devotions, my mind wanders off to a hundred different places. What do I need at the grocery store? What do I have on my agenda today? Did I return those e-mails yet? Many thoughts go through my mind during devotions, but not all of them pertain to God.

Our world today offers such a wide variety of conveniences that we don't feel we should ever have to be still and wait for anything. I can get a hold of people in a flash through my cell phone, e-mail, or texts. In fewer than five minutes, I can get a pizza, a fresh salad, a chicken dinner, or a loaded burrito. At home I can make a skillet meal in fifteen minutes, then put the dishes in my dishwasher, which will clean and sterilize an entire load in fewer than two hours.

I'm so accustomed to getting what I want quickly that the other day I stopped reheating my coffee in the microwave after nineteen seconds because it was taking too much time!

Practicing the discipline of being still can seem strange in an age when we rarely have to pause for anything. However, Psalm 46:10 says, "Be still, and know that I am God." The last time I read this verse I realized something. God doesn't want a percentage of our attention. He wants all of it. When I spend time with God, I need to be fully devoted to Him. I need to be still and to listen. I can succeed in doing this by restructuring my devotional time to include silence.

Sometimes when I pray, I wonder why God doesn't seem to give me an answer. Then I think about how much time I've actually spent with Him, reading the Scriptures and listening for His voice. I am guilty of praying and not hearing. I talk to God, but I don't listen quietly for His response.

Frankly, if we want to hear from heaven, we need to shut up. Please don't tell my kids I said "shut up" or I'll get in big trouble! I'll conclude by rephrasing Psalm 46:10-11 into a prayer.

Prayer: *Lord, I am going to shut up and listen. I acknowledge that You are God. You are more than enough for any situation I encounter, so I will trust You. Part of trusting You is presenting my requests to You, then sitting quietly to listen for Your response. You may not answer immediately, but I realize that there is no chance for me to hear Your answer if I'm not listening! You will be exalted among the nations and You will be exalted on earth. You are that amazing! You, the Lord Almighty, are always with me. You are the God of Jacob and You are my fortress. You have always been around, and You will protect me through any storm in life. Amen.*

Keep a notebook nearby so that when your mind wanders during your devotions, you can write down your thoughts (like your grocery list or the name of someone you forgot to call). Then you can get back to spending time with God. Now take some time to pray and quietly listen for God's voice.

Notes/Prayer Requests & Praises

_____

_____

_____

_____

_____

_____

_____

Week 2

Date 8: How Smart Is That?

Scripture Readings: 1 Kings 10:23-25, 11:1-6

I once read a magazine article about a young man who swindled people out of a lot of money. He ran a Ponzi scheme in the late 1980s at the early age of twenty. He was convicted of fifty-seven federal felonies, sentenced to twenty-five years in prison, and ordered to pay $26 million in restitution.

He later became a Christian, and after he got out of prison, he became a pastor at a church in San Diego, California. He seemed to have turned his life around, and he even helped the government catch criminals involved in the same activities that led him to jail. However, after his amazing story of redemption, this man made the same mistakes a second time.

The headline for this man's life story could read, "From Criminal to Man Reformed to Criminal Again." How smart is that? As I read the article, I was saddened that this man had come so far toward rehabilitating his life just to let poor choices again become his downfall. Then I realized how sad it must make God when I repeatedly make the same mistakes. Every day God gives me the freedom to make choices, and I readily admit that they are not always wise.

In the Old Testament, we see that even Solomon, who was known for his wisdom, struggled with poor choices. First Kings 10 reveals that he became richer and wiser than any other king on earth. People from every nation came to consult with him and to hear the wisdom God had given to him. It sure seemed like King Solomon had it all together—wisdom and wealth besides.

However, as with the man profiled in the magazine, King Solomon's life took a fateful turn. He chose to marry women whom the

Lord had forbidden him to wed. In his old age, they succeeded in turning his heart away from God. The Bible says that Solomon refused to follow the Lord completely as his father, David, had done.

Oh, that I would not make the same mistake as Solomon. I desire to seek God in all aspects of my life so that I will be wise in the knowledge of His truth. I must seek God's Word each day for wisdom to guide me through life. I want the headline for my life story to read, "From Sinner to Saved to Forever Changed." How smart is that?

Prayer: *Lord, when I am tempted to go against Your will and Your Word, please help me to be strong. I want to depend on You and You alone. I want to look to You as the source of my strength to get through each day. Thank You for loving me and for forgiving me when I sin. I want to follow You completely! Amen.*

Think of someone you know who follows the Lord completely. Take time right now to thank the Lord for his or her influence on your life. Take time this week to thank that person through a note, an e-mail, or a phone call.

Notes/Prayer Requests & Praises

_____

_____

_____

_____

_____

_____

Date 9: Running on Empty

Scripture Reading: Colossians 1:24-2:7

It's funny. I would never expect my car to run without gasoline. When the gas tank is low, I fill it up as quickly as I can. I know what would happen if I didn't; my car would stop working and then I would be without transportation. I would never willingly allow that to happen.

A similar concept holds true for people. I once heard someone compare the amount of water in a glass to how we feel about our lives. When our glass is full, we have something to give to others. We can pour a little out and still have something left to satisfy our needs. When our glass is running low, however, every drop of water we pour out deprives our bodies of sustenance.

Some of the things that fill our glass include kind words, time with God, healthy relationships, positive work environments, a healthy church, and encouraging friendships. Some things that drain our glass are bitterness, unforgiveness, stress, busyness, illness, financial troubles, unhealthy relationships, and lack of time with God.

How full is your glass right now? There have been times when my glass has been full to the point of overflowing. During these times, I've been blessed with sufficient mental, emotional, and physical energy to invest in others without draining my glass. Sometimes, however, I have found my glass running on empty.

One day when my glass was nearly dry, I called up a dear friend. I wanted her support and her advice about some issues in my life. She listened thoughtfully as I lamented. When I finished talking, she gave me great advice, then added something that especially filled my glass. She said, "That's a really tough situation." Her simple statement confirmed what I was feeling and showed that she understood my pain. She had poured water into my glass and given me hope that I would get through this time of trial.

Friends provide much-needed support, but I want and need Jesus to be my chief glass filler. One way He fills me up is through Christian speakers and women's retreats. There's comfort in spending time with other women who have the same need and desire to walk through life with God that I do. Another way He fills me up is through my quiet time. I love sitting in His presence as He gently pours water into my glass. When we have the source of living water readily available, there's no reason ever to run on empty!

Prayer: *Jesus, I just want to be found by You. Please fill my glass with You so that I may overflow on those around me. I want to praise You and to love You no matter where life takes me. I love You, and I ask You to fill me with Yourself. Amen.*

How full is your glass right now? If it is running low, make time today for the chief glass filler to satisfy your needs.

Notes/Prayer Requests & Praises

_____

_____

_____

_____

_____

_____

_____

_____

Date 10: From Pagers to Siri

Scripture Reading: 1 Chronicles 14:8-17

One day when my kids were in their early teens, they asked me what kind of cell phones were available when I was growing up. They were stunned when I told them that I didn't have a cell phone growing up. "How did you call people?" they asked. "We had a phone on the wall with push buttons and a cord so long it could stretch into many different rooms," I told them. They looked at me like I was from another planet as they tried to comprehend what I had just said.

It's crazy to contemplate how our methods of communication have changed over the years. This will probably date me a little, but when I got my first job out of college, I was given a pager. My job was to help film video programs about environmental resources, so when I was paged, I was usually in the middle of a forest or a wetland. As you can guess, finding a telephone to call back to work usually took a while.

I remember when I got my first cell phone. Talk about moving up in the world! The direct and immediate communication the cell phone provided was amazing. When I got unlimited texting, I was shocked at how I could text a message and get an instantaneous response. Now I've evolved to an iPhone with Siri. If you ask Siri something, Siri understands what you say, knows what you mean, and even talks back. You can ask Siri, "Where can I find a good cheeseburger?" and Siri will list the restaurants in your area that serve cheeseburgers.

Sometimes we forget we have our own Siri already in place. It's called prayer! Any time of the day or the night, we can call on God and He will answer us. No 4G service is required! Jeremiah 33:3 says, "Call to me and I will answer you and tell you great and unsearchable things you do not know." While modern technology offers great wonders, God will always be first in the communication market!

David and God often had conversations. Think about that for a minute. I'm talking about personal communication with the living God! Here's one example of their dialogues.

"David asked God, 'Should I go out to fight the Philistines? Will you hand them over to me?' The Lord replied, 'Yes, go ahead. I will hand them over to you'" (1 Chronicles 14:10 NLT).

David simply asked God for direction, and God answered him. Now that's better than any pager, text message, or Siri. If man-made Siri can listen and understand you, how much more can the God who created you listen and understand you when you call on Him?

Prayer: *God, You created me and You know me better than any person or phone ever could. I want to keep the lines of communication open between us. I promise to go to You for advice, and I believe that You will listen to me and will answer my prayers. Thank You for caring about me and loving me enough to provide a way for me to talk to You. Amen.*

The next time you're tempted to pick up your cell phone, first say a prayer to God.

Notes/Prayer Requests & Praises

_____

_____

_____

_____

_____

_____

Date 11: Is It More Blessed to Give or to Receive?

Scripture Readings: Acts 20:35; Matthew 10:8; John 1:12; 1 Timothy 1:15-16

One of the first verses I learned as a child was Acts 20:35, "It is more blessed to give than to receive." The message of this verse is an important one—serving others should be an integral part of our daily lives. Scripture reiterates this command, as today's Bible readings show.

Then how can I ask whether it is more blessed to give or to receive?

It is important to give of ourselves, yet it is also important to receive. There are times when we need to receive graciously from others. This is not always an easy thing to do. When others help us, our natural tendency is to want to give back an equal portion of what they've given us.

I once needed to accept help from a friend. She lovingly took many hours out of her busy week to help me with an emergency project at my home. I wanted to make her dinner or buy her a gift certificate to compensate her for the time she spent helping me. When I asked her when I could bring her family dinner, she told me, "Gretchyn, if you bring me dinner I really will be mad at you! Just accept my help and say thank you."

Those were powerful words. It was humbling for me to accept her help and give her nothing in return, but I learned a valuable lesson. Sometimes we are supposed to sacrificially give, and sometimes we are supposed to graciously receive.

Christ offers us the free gift of eternal life, and all we need to do to spend eternity with Him is to receive it. God wants us to receive the gift of His Son. When we accept Jesus into our lives, we naturally start wanting to share His love with others. That's where the giving comes in.

So what's the answer? Is it more blessed to give or to receive? I think that while Scripture tells us it is more blessed to give than to receive, God has asked us to do both.

Prayer: *Lord, Your Word says it is more blessed to give than to receive. I know You want me to share my time and talents to help others. I want to see needs around me and to serve others out of a heart of love for You. I also realize that I need to receive help when others want to bless me. Please show me how to be a sacrificial giver and also a gracious receiver. Amen.*

Is it hard for you to accept help from someone and just say thank you? Take a minute right now to plan what you will say to the next person who pays you a compliment or does something nice for you.

Notes/Prayer Requests & Praises

_____

_____

_____

_____

_____

_____

_____

_____

Date 12: Baby, Baby!

Scripture Reading: Leviticus 23:9-14

I just love baby dedications at church. First, it's fun to watch those cute babies play with our pastor's mustache or squirm in his arms. Second, it's a blessing to support the parents as they commit to raise their children in a Godly home and promise to teach them about Christ's love.

However, what I love most about baby dedications is when the pastor turns to the congregation and asks us if we are ready to live lives that will point these children to the Lord. He asks if we are willing to help these children come to know Jesus in a personal way.

Each baby dedication is a time of reflection for me. It's a time for me to recommit my life to the Lord as I realize that I have an important job to do - not only for my own family - but also for the kids in our congregation and our community. You see, it's not only each family's job to point children to Christ; it's the responsibility of the entire church body.

I've found Leviticus to be a rather strange book to read. It's full of rules for the Israelites. However, one phrase stands out: *generation to generation*. The Lord is clear that what He's commanding is not just for these people at one point in time; it's to be passed on from generation to generation.

Just as the Israelites were responsible for passing on their laws and traditions to future generations, we are responsible for passing on our love for the Lord and knowledge of His Word to the children around us.

There are many ways to encourage kids. You could coach a youth sports team, volunteer at church or in a school classroom, buy lemonade from the kids down the street, write a note of encouragement to a child you know, or attend a program, a school play, or a sporting event to support a child in your community.

I've seen people in my community do all of these things. No matter what your skills or abilities are, even if you don't consider yourself a "kid person," rest assured there is a way for you to affect future generations with Christ's love.

Prayer: *Dear heavenly Father, I know You love children dearly. While Your Son lived on earth, He took extra time to talk to the children whom He met. I want to follow Your example and show extra love to children. Please show me how I can do this. Holy Spirit, please lead me to the area of service where I can help children grow to love You more. I want to live my life so that children have an example of how to love You. Amen.*

This week ask God for a specific way that you can make an impact on future generations.

Notes/Prayer Requests & Praises

_____

_____

_____

_____

_____

_____

_____

_____

Date 13: Misunderstandings

Scripture Reading: James 1

It was Thursday and I was excited because I had plans to meet a friend for dinner that evening. Just to be safe, I texted her to confirm the time and the place we would meet. A few minutes later, my phone rang. It was my friend calling to say she thought we had planned to meet the following Thursday. One of us had gotten the date wrong, creating a misunderstanding.

There are also times when we can misunderstand Scripture. Sometimes we will think a verse means one thing when it really means another.

This happened to me recently as I read the book of James. James 1:5-8 says, "If any of you lacks wisdom, he should ask God, who gives generously to all without finding fault, and it will be given to him. But when he asks, he must believe and not doubt, because he who doubts is like a wave of the sea, blown and tossed by the wind. That man should not think he will receive anything from the Lord; he is a double-minded man, unstable in all he does."

When I was growing up, my class at our Christian school memorized these verses. Unfortunately, I misunderstood their meaning. I used to think James was saying that I should bring my specific requests to God, then believe that He would answer my prayer according to His will. When I read these verses as an adult, I was surprised to realize that I had misunderstood James's message.

In reality, James is telling us that if we need wisdom in our lives, we should ask God for it. These verses don't say that we should ask God to fix our problems, but that we should ask Him for wisdom to deal with them. He promises that He will give us wisdom when we ask, on one condition: we must believe and not doubt.

Lately I've realized the second part of these verses is the harder one for me. I can say I believe God will give me wisdom, but do

I really trust and believe, or do I keep some of the control for myself? I'm a planner and a controller, so I don't like to leave any part of my life up to someone else. But James clearly says that we must ask for wisdom and believe that God will give it to us, or we cannot expect to receive anything from Him.

These are powerful words. Now that I understand their meaning, I am working on putting them into practice. When a challenge arises, I now ask for wisdom to deal with it. Then I tell God I believe He is in control. This is a new concept for me to implement in my life. Now that James has set me straight, I need to learn from my misunderstanding!

Prayer: *Thank You, Lord, for clarifying what Scripture verses mean. I don't want to misunderstand Your Word. Thank You for Your promise that if I ask for wisdom, You will give it to me generously, without finding fault. Please clear up any misunderstandings I might have in my spiritual walk so that I may grow closer to You. Amen.*

Do you feel that you need wisdom in a certain area of your life? Ask God!

Notes/Prayer Requests & Praises

_____

_____

_____

_____

_____

_____

_____

Date 14: One of Those Days

Scripture Reading: Psalm 103

Have you ever experienced a day when nothing seemed to go as planned and you felt like kicking the dog? I have had one of those days, and I'm ashamed to say that I didn't handle it well. I was mad, frustrated, and annoyed with everyone around me. My husband and I had a disagreement, my kids weren't obeying me, and I was beating myself up for not being a good enough friend. I felt worse about myself by the minute.

On the evening of that day, we ran errands as a family. I should have remembered that kids and errands don't always mix well, because this time they were a lethal combination. Even a store clerk had to reprimand my kids. It was not my most shining moment as a parent. By the time we arrived home later that evening, I was mentally exhausted.

My son, however, unaffected by the day's events, still had a bounce in his step. There's nothing more annoying to someone entwined in a mental pity party than cheerfulness. The minute we got out of the car, he ran up to me and excitedly asked, "Mom, can I tell you something?" The "I'm mad at you right now" look in my eyes must have changed his mind because he slowly backed away from me and said, "I'll just tell you about it tomorrow!" Then he turned and ran into the house.

I decided to go on a walk to spend some time with God and process the events of the day. I thought about Psalm 103, which I had read earlier that morning. Verse ten says that God does not treat us as our sins deserve. Verse eleven proclaims that His love for us stretches as high as the heavens.

I realized that my self-imposed inadequacies fade away when God looks at me. It's who I am in Him that matters. I had been focusing on what I thought were my failures instead of looking at myself through God's eyes. I felt God's love wash over me and the painful memories of the day faded in comparison.

Prayer: *Lord, thank You for loving me in spite of my failures and inadequacies. Your love stretches from everlasting to everlasting. Even when I am frustrated with myself and those around me, Your love is always there for me. I need to focus on who I am in You and cling to that beautiful thought. Thank You for extending Your righteousness to my children and someday to my grandchildren. I am blessed by Your perfect love for me and for my family. Amen.*

Think about your most recent bad day. What would have been different about it if you had stepped back and looked at yourself from God's loving perspective?

Notes/Prayer Requests & Praises

_____

_____

_____

_____

_____

_____

_____

_____

_____

Week 3

Date 15: Step Away from the Chocolate

Scripture Reading: Genesis 4:1-12

One day when my daughter was around five years old, she came into my office with a face full of chocolate. We both knew she had not asked permission to eat candy.

Fully knowing the answer, I asked her, "Did you just eat a Milky Way?"

"No," she answered, very seriously. I could see she was holding the wrapper and the uneaten portion of the candy bar in her little hands.

"Then where did you get that?" I asked, pointing toward the candy in her hand.

Without missing a beat, she looked down incredulously at her hand and replied in a shocked voice, "How did *that* get there?"

I still laugh every time I remember this story. While the absurdity of my daughter's comments was humorous, she was traveling down a slippery slope. Her disobedience started with eating the chocolate and continued with a lie to try to cover it up.

There's a similar situation in Genesis 4. Cain, a farmer, presented some of his crops as a gift to God when he should have given the *best* of his crops. In comparison, Cain's brother Abel, a shepherd, offered the best of his firstborn lambs to God.

The Lord accepted Abel's gift, but He did not accept Cain's. This made Cain so angry that he attacked his brother and killed him.

When God asked Cain where Abel was, Cain lied by pretending he didn't know. What had started out with the sin of disobedience had turned into murder and then a lie.

My daughter was foolish to think I wouldn't see the chocolate evidence smeared all over her face, and Cain was foolish to think the Lord wouldn't know he had offered a cheap gift, murdered his brother, and then lied about it. Genesis 4:7 NLT says, "Sin is crouching at the door, eager to control you. But you must subdue it and be its master." If you don't immediately subdue the first appearance of sin in your life, other sins will start to control you.

Don't take that first bite of the Milky Way. God can see the chocolate on your face!

Prayer: *Lord, after reading this passage in Genesis, I can see how one sin breeds other sins. If I fall into sin, it can easily control me and become my master. I want to say no to each sin and temptation in my life. I want to be aware of sin so that I can stop it before it even begins. Amen.*

Is there sin crouching at your door? What one specific area of your life must be subdued before it causes other sins?

Notes/Prayer Requests & Praises

_____

_____

_____

_____

_____

Date 16: It's Not Fair

Scripture Readings: Luke 15:11-32; Ephesians 2:8-9

Today's first reading may be familiar to you. If you grew up going to church, you probably heard it told many times. It's a parable, which is a simple story used to illustrate a spiritual or moral lesson. What comes to your mind when you think about the Parable of the Lost Son?

To be honest, this story has always irked me. That probably isn't what you were expecting me to say. My logical, fair mind can't comprehend this story. Every time I hear it, my mind screams, *It's not fair!* I find myself sympathizing with the Prodigal Son's older brother since it seems like he got a raw deal.

Recently I read this passage during my devotional time. Then I prayed and asked God why this story was included in Scripture. I was stunned by His response. I heard Him say, "I included this parable to show you an example of grace." At last, this story made sense to my logical, narrow mind!

While I had been looking at the story exclusively from the view of the older brother, Jesus had a broader message in mind. The parable was never supposed to be about the unjust treatment of the older brother, but about the grace extended to the younger one. All along I had been missing a valuable lesson because my stubborn, legalistic mind couldn't comprehend the concept of grace.

Grace is God's kindness and mercy given to all sinful humanity. The younger son did not deserve to live in his father's household after running away and wasting his inheritance. The father could have ostracized his son, but instead chose to welcome him back home. That's a beautiful example of grace!

God has given us grace, as Ephesians 2:8-9 notes. Just as the younger son did nothing to deserve his father's favor, so we can do nothing to deserve our heavenly Father's favor. God's grace is a free gift. It is generously given to us, and we must choose whether to accept it and whether we will extend it to others.

We need grace for the friend who has hurt us yet again. We need grace for the spouse who lets us down. We need grace to accept and to love a difficult family member. We need grace for ourselves when we make a mistake.

When I think about grace, I realize that it's not fair. However, that's the part that makes it so amazing!

Prayer: *Heavenly Father, I admit that sometimes it is hard to extend grace. Please take my human inadequacies and help me be more like You. I want to accept Your grace and give it to others so that they may see You more clearly. Amen.*

Is there someone in your life who needs grace? Maybe it's you. Make an effort this week to extend grace to this person or to yourself.

Notes/Prayer Requests & Praises

_____

_____

_____

_____

_____

_____

_____

Date 17: Pick Up Your Coffee and Follow Him

Scripture Reading: John 1:35-51

Imagine yourself casually strolling along the streets of a quaint town. You are window-shopping while enjoying your favorite hot drink. (Mine's a white chocolate latte.) As you stop to glance at a boutique, you suddenly realize there is someone beside you. As you turn to face Him, you see a kind man searching your face as if He knows you.

"I've wanted to speak with you since I saw you get your coffee," He says.

"Do I know you?" you ask, unafraid but a little perplexed.

"You know Me, but we haven't met in person. My name is Jesus, and I want you to put down your coffee and follow Me." He says this so matter-of-factly that you immediately set down your drink and walk with Him. Others are following this man, too, and you suddenly realize this is Jesus Christ, the Son of God and the King of Israel.

This is a modern-day illustration of how Jesus called His disciples in John 1:35-51. Andrew, Peter, and Philip followed Jesus without hesitation, but Nathanael waivered. I can relate more to Nathanael than to the other three who followed so quickly. Change doesn't come easily for me, and I don't think it was effortless for Nathanael either.

Nathanael needed a little confirmation before he would take the plunge and follow Jesus. "How do You know me?" Nathanael questioned. Jesus answered, "I saw you while you were sitting under the fig tree before Philip called you." Jesus knew all about Nathanael before He even met him. This intimate knowledge convinced Nathanael, and he replied, "Rabbi, You are the Son of God; You are the King of Israel."

Let's look at the other disciples in this passage. They followed Jesus without question from the beginning. The disciples quit what they were doing and left with Jesus because they could tell there was something special about Him. They wanted to know more, so they dropped everything to follow Him.

I feel the same way today as the disciples did two thousand years ago. The more I dig into the Bible, the more I want to learn about Jesus. There is something amazing about Him that draws me in today just as it drew in the disciples so long ago.

The best part of my day is sitting on the far left side of my favorite couch with a hot cup of coffee, reading the Bible and getting to know more about the Lord. It's ironic that I am usually not setting down my coffee to follow Jesus but picking it up!

Prayer: *Dear King of Israel, thank You for caring about me so much that You want to spend time with me. I want to make time for You each day to get to know You better. Amen.*

Describe your favorite place to spend time with God.

Notes/Prayer Requests & Praises

_____

_____

_____

_____

_____

_____

Date 18: Why Do We Have Big Buts?

Scripture Readings: Exodus 3, 4

Moses had a big *but*. Actually, Moses had three big buts. Before this devotional starts going downhill, let me explain what I mean.

In Exodus 3, God revealed Himself to Moses in the form of a burning bush. That in itself is an amazing feat, and yet Moses seemed unimpressed. When the Lord told Moses (through the fiery bush) that He wanted him to lead the Israelites out of Egypt, Moses basically replied, "But God ..."

His first *but* came when he asked God, "Who am I, that I should go to Pharaoh and bring the Israelites out of Egypt?" God patiently responded, "I will be with you."

Moses had a second *but*. He asked God, "What should I do if the people ask me who sent me?" God definitively answered, "Tell them, I AM has sent me to you." The Lord followed this statement with specific instructions and a well-laid plan for Moses to follow.

Even after hearing this plan and seeing God appear through a burning bush, Moses had another *but*. He said, "But God, I'm not a good public speaker."

One morning I nervously anticipated an appointment to speak at a women's group. I had a list of *buts* running through my mind before I left home. But I'm not good at speaking in public. But the women might think I'm boring, weird, or even nuts (though this may actually be true). But I might not connect with them. Lots of big *buts*!

That morning the Lord showed me the same answer He gave Moses thousands of years earlier after his third *but*. "Who gave man his mouth? Who makes him deaf or mute? Who gives him sight or makes him blind? Is it not I, the Lord? Now *go; I will help you speak and will teach you what to say*" (Exodus 4:11-12, emphasis mine).

I got in my car and left! How could I say no when God promised to meet my needs by helping me speak and telling me what to say? God wants to turn our *buts* into "You can do it through Me!"

Prayer: *Lord, thank You for Your promises of support, which are just as valid today as they were many years ago. You have proven that You love me and will always carry me through difficult situations. Thank You for being a God who is compassionate and patient with me. You are amazing and wonderful! Amen.*

What is the *but* in your life right now?

Notes/Prayer Requests & Praises

_____

_____

_____

_____

_____

_____

_____

_____

_____

Date 19: Ten Bad Days

Scripture Reading: Isaiah 55

On a recent trip I met a remarkable bellman. He was one of those people who exude positive energy, and I could feel that energy the minute he stepped on the elevator with me.

As we rode together, he told me about his job and why it was important for him to do it with excellence. He explained that if people didn't like the service at the hotel, they wouldn't come back. I could tell he cared about doing his job well.

He was one of the most upbeat people I'd ever met, even though his job must have included dealing with crabby customers each day. He could have greeted me with a pleasant hello, yet he chose to go a step further. He struck up a friendly conversation with me and made my day a little brighter. The smile on his face radiated enthusiasm for life.

As we exited the elevator, he stepped aside and told me his secret. He said he allowed himself to have only ten bad days a year! He said that when one of his days started to head down a negative path, he stopped to decide whether he wanted to use up one of his bad days. After thinking it over, he often ended up changing his attitude.

I felt God prompting me to continue the conversation, so I explained that I believed God was in charge of all of our good days and bad days.

His face brightened and he enthusiastically agreed with me. I could tell that there was a deeper, more spiritual reason behind his happiness.

This man's positive approach could work for anyone. Bad situations might not look so bleak if we allowed ourselves just ten bad days per year. Taking this approach could change our lives. It would force us to reprioritize. And we would have at least 355 good days a year!

Prayer: *Lord, I want to go out in joy each day, just as You suggest in Isaiah 55:12. I want to live my life in the joy of Your salvation. I want to thank You for all You've done for me and to choose to live my life in appreciation of Your love. I want to exude Your love so that others may see that You are the reason for the smile on my face and for my positive attitude. Amen.*

How do you think your attitude would differ if you allowed yourself ten bad days per year? When you're having a tough day and your frustration level soars, ask yourself if you're willing to use up one of your ten allotted bad days.

Notes/Prayer Requests & Praises

_____

_____

_____

_____

_____

_____

_____

_____

_____

_____

Date 20: May I Give You a Pedicure?

Scripture Reading: John 13:1-17

Have you ever had a pedicure? If you have, then you know how heavenly this feels. But have you ever thought about the people giving pedicures? Their job is to wash dirty, sweaty, smelly, calloused, ugly feet. They soak, scrub, buff, sand, and clip something dirty into something clean.

When Jesus lived on earth, washing a guest's feet was a job for a household servant. Imagine how dirty feet were back in Bible times. A servant must have scraped layer upon layer of dirt from a guest's feet. Even the posture of cleaning feet—bending low—displays humility.

Knowing these cultural facts makes it even more surprising to read in John 13 that Jesus washed His disciples' feet. He lowered Himself to the position of a servant. What were the disciples feeling when their Lord and teacher humbly washed their filthy feet?

When Jesus finished the Bible-era pedicure, He said, "Now that I have washed your feet, you should wash one another's feet ... I tell you the truth, no servant is greater than his master."

Jesus was telling His disciples in no uncertain terms that they should serve others. We also must accept this call. Does this mean we should go from house to house with a basin of warm water and some foot scrub? While our neighbors would probably love it, Jesus meant that we should serve others according to their needs.

Serving others can take many forms. You can pray, send a note, bring a meal, donate your time, go on a mission trip, give financially, watch someone's kids, help at a homeless shelter, become a foster parent—the list could go on forever. There are millions of ways to "wash feet"!

Whose "feet" does God want you to wash? How does God want you to give a "pedicure" to someone in need? Follow Christ's example and wash someone's feet today.

Prayer: *Jesus, thank You for setting the example of serving others by washing Your disciples' feet. I want to follow Your command to serve others. Please show me a need that I can meet. I want to humbly serve others. I want to wash feet. Amen.*

Is God prompting you with a specific way to wash someone's feet? If not, pray that He will bring someone to mind whom you can bless.

Notes/Prayer Requests & Praises

_____

_____

_____

_____

_____

_____

_____

_____

Date 21: Pick Me!

Scripture Readings: 1 Corinthians 6:19-20; John 1:12

A few years ago, my husband and I went on a company trip to Miami Beach, Florida. This was not my first choice for a vacation destination, but we were thankful for the chance to get away.

After arriving, we learned that our hotel housed one of the premier nightclubs in the area. We are not clubbers, but one night we decided to hang out in the hotel lobby to people watch.

What we saw was a world apart from the night life we were used to in rural Minnesota! We were surrounded by micro-miniskirts, tight tops, and perfectly made-up faces. These gorgeous young ladies were all trying to be beautiful for one reason—to gain access to the club. We watched as they waited in line for a chance to enter. We heard that once you got in, there was a two-hundred-dollar cover charge and drinks cost three hundred dollars! I also heard that eight hundred dollars would pay for the right to sit on a couch.

I think I paid less than eight hundred for the couch in my living room—and I got to keep it!

What made me even sadder than watching people spend crazy amounts of money on short-lived entertainment was watching how they gained admission to the club. "Scouts" would search the hotel lobby for "beautiful people." When someone caught his eye, a scout would tap the candidate on the shoulder, then lead the person to the front of the line and into the club.

As I watched this scene unfold, a thought entered my mind. I envisioned God as one of those scouts. I pictured Him searching the room, stopping next to me, then tapping me on the shoulder. He picked me! Then I pictured Him tapping all the people in the room, giving everyone access to the greatest club in the world—heaven!

I'm so glad that God accepts me for who I am. He accepts you, too. He doesn't care about what you look like or what you've done.

Jesus paid our cover charge when He died on the cross. He's tapped every one of us on the shoulder and offered us not just one night with Him, but eternity. All we have to do is follow Him to the front of the line. The price has been paid.

Prayer: *Lord, thank You for accepting me for who I am and for not judging me on my outward appearance. Thank You for looking at my heart. Thank You for paying my debt when You sent Your Son to die on the cross. Amen.*

Optional prayer to accept the gift of Jesus: *Dear God, I believe in You and want to be Your child. I am sorry for my sins and ask Your forgiveness. I believe that You sent Your Son Jesus to die on the cross for my sins. Please take control of my life. I realize that You can do a better job than I can! I promise to get to know You better as I seek You each day. Amen.*

Have you accepted God's gift of eternal life? He is tapping on your shoulder, so what is holding you back?

Notes/Prayer Requests & Praises

_____

_____

_____

_____

_____

_____

Week 4

Date 22: Facts or Feelings?

Scripture Reading: Ruth 1

One night I spoke to a group of fourth- and fifth-grade girls about the book of Ruth, which is loaded with emotions. I mentioned that as females, we experience many emotions. I was surprised to watch most of the girls nod their heads in agreement. Even girls as young as nine and ten understood the power of feelings in their lives.

Unfortunately, feelings are not always based on facts. Naomi, whose story is told in the book of Ruth, wrestled with the conflict between facts and feelings.

Naomi experienced many situations that would leave anyone discouraged. Because of a famine in her homeland, she was forced to move to a new land with her husband and her two sons. In this new land, her sons got married, but then her husband and sons died. Finally, many years later, the famine in her homeland ended and Naomi decided to return. The one bright spot in her life was her daughter-in-law Ruth, who chose to leave her familiar surroundings and to move with Naomi.

However, despite this blessing, Naomi focused on her negative feelings. She said, "Don't call me Naomi [which means "pleasant"] ... call me Mara, because the Almighty has made my life very bitter. I went away full, but the Lord has brought me back empty. Why call me Naomi? The Lord has afflicted me; the Almighty has brought misfortune upon me" (Ruth 1:20-21).

Sometimes when things don't go as planned, people have a tendency to exaggerate. This is what Naomi seems to have done. She had every right to be frustrated with how her life had played out, but she appears to have ignored the facts and based her conclusions solely on her feelings.

- Naomi felt that her life was bitter. The fact was that she was back in her hometown with family and friends.
- Naomi felt that the Lord had brought her back empty. The fact was that her loyal daughter-in-law, Ruth, was with her.
- Naomi felt that the Lord had afflicted her. The fact was that the Lord did not cause her husband and her sons to die.

Like Naomi, all of us struggle with negative thoughts and feelings from time to time. When you're going through a tough time, it's important to think realistically about the situation to determine if your struggle is based on facts or on feelings.

Prayer: *Lord, thank You for Scripture that focuses my mind on facts. Philippians 4:8 says, "Finally, brothers, whatever is **true**, whatever is **noble**, whatever is **right**, whatever is **pure**, whatever is **lovely**, whatever is **admirable**—if anything is **excellent** or **praiseworthy**—think about such things." Amen.*

Choose two of the bolded words from Philippians 4:8 and look up their definitions to learn more about the "facts" God wants for your life.

Notes/Prayer Requests & Praises

_____

_____

_____

_____

_____

Date 23: Thursdays with Wayne

Scripture Reading: James 1:2-5

I will never forget the first Thursday I spent with Wayne. He and I were two very different people, but we had one thing in common—time. My kids were both in school, so I had spare time during the day. Wayne had ALS—Lou Gehrig's disease—and had just stopped working, which freed up his daily schedule. When I found out that Wayne needed help a few hours a week, I decided to volunteer for the job.

At first I thought the situation might be awkward—a stay-at-home mom fixing lunch for a middle-aged man. I also thought conversation could be strained. Would we talk about his illness or would there be an elephant in the room? I soon found there was no cause for worry, because Wayne made me feel right at home the minute I walked in his door. His surprising candor about his illness and imminent death stomped out any elephant I could have imagined.

When I started helping Wayne, we decided to read books together. We read a few Christian books, but we usually did more talking than reading. It was hard to get much reading in when I asked a lot of questions and Wayne told a lot of stories.

As Wayne's illness progressed, our time together grew from a few hours at a stretch to a full day. We would drink coffee and eat breakfast and lunch. Then Wayne would rest and I would go home. When we weren't eating a meal or drinking coffee, we would "discuss." I loved to listen to Wayne share his unique perspective on life. I admired how courageously he lived his life and always had a positive attitude, even though he had every right to be negative about the cruel disease that was ravaging his body.

God allowed both good and bad things into Wayne's life during our time together. I watched him closely and was amazed that he never blamed God or wished that his life was different. I hope if I am ever in a situation like that, I will be as faithful to God as Wayne was.

It was a bittersweet day when Wayne went to meet Jesus. I was sad to lose a friend, but I was thrilled that he would no longer be in pain. My final Thursday with Wayne was the day of his funeral, or celebration of life. On that day, we celebrated a life well-lived. We honored a brave man who stared a horrible disease in the face and fought back with all of his might. I celebrated my friend and brother in Christ. I will always remember the precious gift he gave me—the gift of Thursdays, the gift of his time.

Prayer: *Heavenly Father, thank You for the gift of time. Please help me to remember that my time can be given as a gift to others. Help me to leave time in my schedule to be there for others. Thank You for the example Wayne set as he was faithful to You during both the good and the bad times he experienced. Blessed be the name of the Lord. Amen.*

Do you have the gift of time to share with someone? If so, what can you do with that gift?

Notes/Prayer Requests & Praises

_____

_____

_____

_____

_____

_____

Date 24: Because God Says So!

Scripture Reading: Psalm 41

One day as I was walking in Minneapolis with some friends, we passed a homeless man who asked us for spare change. While most of us looked away and ignored him, one of my friends walked over and gave him some money. Her act of kindness taught us a valuable lesson: God wants us to help others, not walk by them.

I was humbled by that experience. In the past I had walked or driven past people who asked for money. It's not that I didn't care about them. It's more that I didn't care enough to help them. My heart hurt for people who had no place to live and were surviving on spare change. My hands, however, did not bear any of the fruit of my heart.

After graduating from college, I worked in downtown Minneapolis and saw people asking for money every day. I became calloused to their needs. I justified the fact that I walked right past them by telling myself these people with their tin cans or guitars looked perfectly capable of getting a job. Maybe they were just lazy. Maybe they hadn't made good use of their money while they had it, so why should I be responsible for helping them out of a crisis?

Why? Because God says so!

Psalm 41:1 says, "Blessed is he who has regard for the weak; the Lord delivers him in times of trouble." God wants our generosity to reflect His own free giving. As He has blessed us, so we should bless others. Now that's something to wrap my little brain around! He has given me more than enough earthly blessings, and on top of that I have the promise of eternal life with Him. With that in mind, I feel humbled when I think of how many needy people I've walked past in my life.

A few months after I was in the city with my friends, my husband and I celebrated our wedding anniversary in Minneapolis. We took a little time to people watch after dinner. It was fun to see the diversity of people enjoying the city that evening. As we sat on a bench, a homeless man approached me and asked for a quarter. I followed my first instinct and told him I didn't have a quarter, but as he walked away I felt the Holy Spirit convicting me.

I realized that it was time I stopped just feeling bad for people in need and actually did something to help. I called out to stop him. As he turned around, I reached into my purse and found some money. It was only a couple of dollars, but he seemed grateful. I realized that it didn't matter why he was homeless or how he got to that place in life. I needed to help others for the sole reason that God says so in His Word.

Prayer: *Lord, help me not only to see the needs of others around me, but to do something about those needs! Please show me how I can help someone today. Amen.*

Make a point of doing something nice for someone in need this week, even if it's as simple as opening the door for someone with a stroller.

Notes/Prayer Requests & Praises

_____

_____

_____

_____

_____

_____

_____

Date 25: Searching for Refuge

Scripture Readings: Psalms 57, 59, 61

One summer my mom and I took my kids up to Minnesota's captivating North Shore to enjoy the breathtaking views of the beautiful rocky shoreline. It was raining as we left, and the rain continued throughout our trip home. As we reached my mom's house to drop her off, the rain's intensity increased and so did my desire for the kids and me to reach our own home and our own beds.

A few minutes after we left Mom's house, the weather turned ugly. I have never driven through such a terrifying storm as I did that day. I could not see even one foot in front of me in the driving rain, and then it began to hail. When I saw lightning flash three times on the road in front of me, I knew the kids and I needed to pray.

I searched for a place on the side of the road to pull over. I longed for any driveway or side road where we could take refuge. If we pulled over on the main road, we risked having someone hit us from behind. If we turned around to go back to my parents' house, we risked having someone coming from the other direction hit us. It was one of the scariest moments of my life.

"We're going to turn around. Pray!" I told the kids. With a desperate prayer, I swung the car around and started the scary journey back to my parents' home. After fifteen long minutes that felt like hours, we arrived at our place of refuge. It felt so good to be safe in a warm, dry place.

I was reminded of this scary instance recently when I read the Psalms in today's Scripture reading. Quite a few of these verses portray God as our Refuge.

"For in You my soul takes refuge. I will take refuge in the shadow of your wings until the disaster has passed" (Psalm 57:1).

"For You are my fortress, my refuge in times of trouble" (Psalm 59:16).

"For You have been my refuge, a strong tower against the foe. I long to dwell in Your tent forever and take refuge in the shelter of Your wings" (Psalm 61:3-4).

These are just a few verses about God being our refuge. There are plenty more on this theme. That day in the midst of a physical storm, God was there, guiding my car to a safe place of refuge. He is also there during emotional storms. The Bible says we can take refuge in the shadow of His wings.

No matter what kind of storm you're experiencing, take refuge in God. He wants to put His arms around you and embrace you. He wants you to take refuge in the shadow of His wings until the storm has passed. Like me on that horrible night, you might have to go through the storm first, but take heart in knowing He will be right beside you until the danger has passed.

Prayer: *Lord, I do not enjoy going through storms, whether they're physical or emotional. However, I know storms are part of life here on earth. Thank You for being such a loving and caring God. Thank You for promising to be my refuge until the storm has passed. Thank You for coming alongside of me as I encounter storms in life. I will trust in You. Amen.*

What storm has God brought you through in your lifetime? Take time now to thank Him for His faithfulness!

Notes/Prayer Requests & Praises

_____

_____

_____

_____

_____

Date 26: Don't Miss Your Opportunity

Scripture Readings: John 16:5-15; Galatians 6:9-10

I admit it's pathetic, but it took me a long time to get over the Minnesota Vikings' NFC championship loss in 2010. Yes, I know it's been a long time since that game was played. Yes, I know multiple Super Bowls have come and gone. I know I should be over the loss by now, but I'm not!

When I think about why I just can't get over that game, I realize my frustration stems from one thing—missed opportunities. Fumbles, bad coaching, and the disturbing interception thrown by a veteran quarterback could all be considered missed opportunities. I'm sure the Vikings would like to have those plays back, but that's not going to happen. They missed their chance to play in the Super Bowl.

Recently, the topic of missed opportunities came up in a conversation with some friends. We talked about how, at one time or another, we felt the Holy Spirit nudging us to do something but we didn't obey. We talked about times when we felt called to send a card, bring a meal, or pray over someone in need, but we didn't do it. We all felt like we had missed openings to help others. I am guilty of making excuses for not obeying the Spirit's prompting. I'll say to myself, *I'm too tired. I'm a bad cook. I'm too busy.*

Once I received an opportunity when I felt the Lord prompting me to call a friend from my Bible class. When I asked her if she was enjoying the study, there was a long pause. She replied, "Actually, I just decided a few minutes ago that I wasn't going to come to the study anymore." When I asked her why, she said that she felt she had too many questions and that everyone else seemed to know more than she did. I assured her that none of us had all the answers and that we were all seeking to know God better. After we talked a little longer, she decided to continue attending the study.

I hung up the phone and immediately thanked God for His perfect timing. I was glad that He had prompted me to call at the exact time my friend had decided to stop attending the study. This experience gave me a glimpse of the Holy Spirit's mighty power.

The best way to recognize an opportunity is by reading God's Word and listening to the Holy Spirit. When you feel His prompting, go for it! Galatians 6:9 says, "Let us not become weary in doing good, for at the proper time we will reap a harvest if we do not give up." What opportunity is God sending your way this week? Don't miss it!

Prayer: *Dear God, thank You for sending the Holy Spirit to guide me. Your Word says that the Holy Spirit is my Counselor and Advocate. I want to listen carefully to Him and follow His prompting. Amen.*

Take time right now to pray. Be still and listen for the Holy Spirit's voice. Then do whatever He is leading you to do!

Notes/Prayer Requests & Praises

_____

_____

_____

_____

_____

_____

_____

Date 27: Panic Mode

Scripture Reading: Ecclesiastes 4:9-12

I vividly remember a time in my life when I was freaking out. My husband and I were going to Florida in two months, and we needed someone to watch our kids. Suddenly one Monday, I started to panic. I needed to find six nights of child care, and for some reason, I needed to do it that Monday.

Do you ever have days like that—days when something that isn't an emergency all of a sudden seems extremely important? That's how it was for me that Monday. I was feeling a sense of urgency about finding a temporary home for my kids, and I quickly worked myself into panic mode.

I tried not to sound as desperate as I felt when I e-mailed a few friends. I hoped that if each of them could take my kids for a night or two, maybe things would work out.

Soon I got a phone call from a friend saying that my kids could stay with her family for the whole week. A couple of hours later, I got an e-mail from another friend who had already rearranged her work schedule and who also offered to take my kids for the entire week. I was shocked!

Still reeling from my friends' generous offers, I headed over to the school for parent orientation night. I saw another friend I had contacted earlier that day. She asked me if I had read my e-mails that night. I told her I hadn't. She said, "You may want to read them. I sent you one that details why our family should get to watch your kids for the whole week."

Again, I was speechless and amazed. My first thought was, *God is so good.* I was overwhelmed by the knowledge that the God who created the universe was so concerned about me that He had found child care for my kids. Now that was a caring God!

I sat through the orientation, but I don't remember hearing much of what the teacher said. My heart was so full of love and thankfulness that I could barely focus on what was happening around me.

It's funny how earlier that morning I was in panic mode. Then God, in His infinite love and mercy, decided to bless me—and not just bless me, but overwhelm me! All I could do was stand in awe of Him and fall more in love with Him.

Prayer: *God, You fill my cup and not just to the top, but to overflowing! Thank You for friends who lift me up and encourage me by their selfless actions. God, You bless me beyond measure. Amen.*

What in your life right now is causing you to panic? Give it over to God!

Notes/Prayer Requests & Praises

_____

_____

_____

_____

_____

_____

_____

_____

Date 28: He Makes Me Feel Safe

Scripture Readings: Psalm 18:2, 62:5-8

Recently I was listening to a young woman talk about her husband. Someone asked why she was attracted to him and what she liked about him. Her response was simple. "He makes me feel safe," she replied. Her words resonated with me because I think that we all want to feel safe.

I remember a time when I did not feel safe. The reason may seem trivial to some people, but anyone with a phobia will relate to my predicament. I thought I heard a mouse in the house. Some people are scared of snakes, others of spiders, but I'm petrified of mice and other rodents. Stuart Little? Not cute. Jerry (of *Tom and Jerry*)? Not cute. Remy, the rat chef in *Ratatouille*? Not even a little cute.

So when I thought I heard a mouse in my house that day, I sat paralyzed on my stairs. My pride evaporated as I called my friend next door, and she came over with her five-year-old son to help me look for the mouse. While her son sat on the stairs with me, my friend searched but could find not even a hint of mouse droppings. Only then did I feel safe enough to get off of the stairs and look for myself.

"Mouse!" yelled her son from his perch on the stairs. My heart stopped beating as I looked at him for a clue as to where the mouse was. "Just kidding," he said, doubling over in laughter. Not funny or cute!

I'm a little embarrassed to say that the mouse noise I thought I heard was really my ice cube maker frantically trying to produce ice. Once the mystery was solved, my dear friend and her "hilarious" son went home. I thanked her for helping me feel safe in my house again.

I realize that many people are going through situations that are much more critical than a mouse in the house. You may feel open, vulnerable, and in need of a safe place to wait out the storm you're enduring.

Many verses in Scripture proclaim that "God is our refuge," so I looked up the word *refuge* in the dictionary. It means "1) The state of being protected, as from danger or hardship; 2) A place that provides protection or shelter: haven; 3) Something to which one may turn for help, relief, or escape." [1]

In the midst of your trials, God wants to be your protector, your shelter, your escape. Will you tuck yourself under God's shelter today? Will you let Him be your protector and trust that He will do what He's promised? He is the only one who can help you feel safe amid turmoil.

Prayer: *Lord, when trials and scary situations enter my life, I am thankful that I can turn to You for protection and guidance. I trust You to get me through the difficult times. Life brings many ups and downs, but I know that You are constant through it all. Amen.*

What trial do you need to trust God with today?

Notes/Prayer Requests & Praises

_____

_____

_____

_____

_____

[1]   *Webster's II New College Dictionary*, s.v. "refuge."

Week 5

Date 29: Statue Obsession

Scripture Reading: 2 Chronicles 29, 30

My kids think I'm weird just because I'm obsessed with Abraham Lincoln. Seriously, though, what's not to like about Honest Abe, the tall man in the black hat? His list of accomplishments includes serving as the sixteenth president of the United States, helping to abolish slavery in America, and consistently standing up for what he believed was right. So when we visited Washington, DC, on a family trip, how could my kids possibly consider it weird that I nearly fainted at the sight of the Lincoln Memorial? I must admit that I was a little surprised myself at how the statue of a man who lived nearly 150 years ago evoked such strong feelings of respect and admiration.

Second Chronicles tells us about a man of character in Judah, King Hezekiah. This guy wasn't afraid to blaze a new trail, and he didn't waste any time doing it! The Bible says that in the first month of his reign, Hezekiah reopened and repaired the temple of the Lord. He was bold enough to start his new job by implementing immediate changes.

The people of Judah had abandoned the Lord and His dwelling place. Hezekiah realized that the Lord's anger had fallen on Judah and Jerusalem for this very reason. He desired to restore Judah to a right relationship with God.

Just like Lincoln, Hezekiah was a leader who wasn't afraid to get his hands dirty. He immediately made sure that the temple was cleansed and that the Levites were purified. He commanded that a burnt offering and sin offering should be made for all of Israel.

Reading this passage, I watched the people's hearts change as they followed Hezekiah's lead in praising God. As the people gave their offerings to God, they underwent a spiritual renewal. The king and all the people bowed down in worship, praising the Lord with psalms. Their hearts became open to God.

I thank God for men and women of character who stand up for what they know is right. Stories like those of Lincoln and Hezekiah inspire me to be bold and courageous. Now please excuse me as I suddenly feel like sitting in my favorite chair, putting on my tall, black hat, and reading a good book about Honest Abe. I have no idea why my kids think I'm obsessed!

Prayer: *Lord God, thank You for preserving the records of people who have boldly followed You. Thank You for the inspiration these people provide. Please show me how I can be bold for You today. May I recognize the opportunity to change my family, my town, and even my world for Your glory. I want to make the most of the opportunities You place in my life. Amen.*

Which people inspire you to stand up for what you believe? Thank God for what their example has meant in your life.

Notes/Prayer Requests & Praises

_____

_____

_____

_____

_____

_____

_____

Date 30: Okay, I Get It!

Scripture Reading: Psalm 62

Over the course of a few days, I got the distinct feeling that God was trying to tell me something. My Scripture reading had consistently focused on the concept of God as my refuge. Then I wrote a blog entry about God being my shelter during the storms of life. Finally, my sister-in-law from Texas mentioned that her church was working on a women's retreat about refuge.

It took me a few days, but eventually a bell went off in my head and I thought, *Okay, I get it! God is trying to show me something!*

To get a better handle on the fact that God wants to be your place of refuge, read the following verses and circle every mention of a word relating to refuge. The psalmist lists synonyms for *refuge* such as *fortress, rock,* and *shield.*

"The Lord is my rock, my fortress and my deliverer; my God is my rock, in whom I take refuge, He is my shield and the horn of my salvation, my stronghold" (Psalm 18:2).

"O my Strength, I watch for You; You, O God, are my fortress" (Psalm 59:9).

"Find rest, O my soul, in God alone; my hope comes from Him, He alone is my rock and my salvation; He is my fortress, I will not be shaken, my salvation and my honor depend on God; He is my mighty rock, my refuge. Trust Him at all times, O people; pour out your hearts to Him, for God is our refuge" (Psalm 62:5-8).

Now list each synonym you found for *refuge.* Here is my list: *rock, fortress, deliverer, shield,* and *strength.* Do we have the same list? These words attest to a powerful God, don't they? I'm so grateful for a persistent God who continually reveals His truths until I get it!

Prayer: *Lord, thank You for pursuing me until I understand the lesson You are trying to teach me. I'm sorry for the times when You have had to repeat that lesson! I want to focus on You so that I can clearly hear Your voice. Amen.*

Take time to read Psalm 62 again, and ask God what lesson He wants you to learn.

Notes/Prayer Requests & Praises

_____

_____

_____

_____

_____

_____

_____

_____

_____

_____

_____

_____

Date 31: Sit in the Dirt

Scripture Reading: Job 1-2:13

A friend once told me that her church's small-group meeting took place at a wake for a member's dad. Small-group meetings usually include snacks, games, dinner, and Bible studies, so I was a little taken aback when she told me that members went to a wake!

She said that the group's attendance at the wake meant a lot to the person whose dad had passed away. Members had shown support and love for their friend, who had just experienced a tough loss.

Through this situation, I was reminded that we don't always have to say exactly the right words to someone who's struggling. Sometimes it's enough for us to be a listening ear. It's enough just to be there for that person.

Reading the book of Job, I recalled that he was a man who had lost everything. He lost not only his possessions, but the people most dear to him. He also suffered with terrible boils from head to toe. This man had gone about as low as anyone could go.

Amid his grieving and suffering, three of Job's friends decided to comfort and to console him. Scripture says that when they saw Job from a distance, they hardly recognized him.

The next part of the story is poignant. Job 2:12 says they wailed loudly, tore their robes, and threw dust over their heads. Then it says they sat on the ground with Job for seven days and nights! Can you imagine sitting with someone and grieving with him for seven days? I love what the next verse says: "No one said a word to Job, for they saw that his suffering was too great for words" (Job 2:13 NLT).

Don't you get a kick out of that picture? Imagine four grown men sitting on the dirty ground in torn clothing, probably smelly after not bathing for seven days. Now that's sympathy! I especially love the fact that they didn't say a word. Of course if they were women, they might have lasted only an hour or so without talking!

This story is a good example for us. When people around us are hurting, we don't have to know exactly what to say, but we can listen. Being there can be enough. It's a liberating concept for me, since I've been known to say the wrong thing more than once. As someone once told me, your presence can be your present.

Prayer: *Lord, it's hard to watch people I care about suffer. I want to fix their problems so they don't have to hurt anymore. However, You have shown me through the example of Job and his friends that sometimes I just need to be available to listen and let You do the rest. Help me to trust in You to meet my needs and the needs of others. Amen.*

Is there someone in your life right now who needs your presence?

Notes/Prayer Requests & Praises

_____

_____

_____

_____

_____

_____

_____

Date 32: A Little Humor

Scripture Reading: Proverbs 30

If you think God doesn't have a sense of humor, I'd encourage you to reconsider. I will offer a personal episode that happened the other day as proof.

The episode took place on the tennis courts in my town on a day when everyone who owned a racquet seemed to be playing tennis. A high school girl and I had almost finished warming up when the embarrassing event occurred. As I lunged for a backhand, the outside of my shoe caught on the court and my ankle twisted. I fell to the ground awkwardly in front of what I perceived to be crowds of people.

The smart choice would have been to go home and elevate my foot with ice packed firmly around my swollen ankle. But I don't always do the smart thing. I didn't want to quit playing, so I limped around the courts for another half hour in front of all the people who had just watched me fall. They probably thought I was nuts—and they were right!

The truth is that I often get injured, and if I sat out every time I fell or hurt myself, I might never actually do anything. I guess that's just the risk I choose to take because I like to play sports, but I'm also accident-prone.

The following morning, as I read my devotions, I thought, *Wouldn't it be funny if somehow there were a Scripture passage related to my incident?* Imagine my surprise when I read this verse:

"I am too stupid to be human, and I lack common sense" (Proverbs 30:2 NLT).

The author of this proverb, a man named Agur, perfectly explained how I felt about my episode the previous day. I felt stupid that I'd fallen in front of everyone. If misery loves company, then stupidity must love it too, because I felt comfort in the fact that Agur had the same feelings as I did. He went on to say that there is only one who has mastered human wisdom. God created each of us uniquely, even those of us who are accident-prone.

If I don't laugh at myself, then who will? (Don't answer that question! I'm sure I could find a lot of people to take that spot.) The point is that it's important not to take ourselves too seriously. God created us with a sense of humor. He has one and so should we!

Prayer: *Dear God, thank You for the gift of laughter. Sometimes I wish laughter didn't come at my expense, but I thank You all the same! Please help me to see the humor in life even in the pain. Thank You for how You made me. You made all of us with Your awesome power. Amen.*

When was the last time you doubled over in a full belly laugh? I hope that remembering why you laughed just brought another smile to your face!

Notes/Prayer Requests & Praises

_____

_____

_____

_____

_____

_____

_____

Date 33: God Is God

Scripture Reading: Exodus 3:1-14

Today's title could be a lesson in stating the obvious. To say that God is God seems like saying that grass is green or clouds are white. However, sometimes it can be hard to fully trust Him when we can't look ahead and see the outcome of His plan.

In the summer of 2012, I traveled to Ukraine on a mission trip. Our team worked at a summer camp that provided orphans and street kids with a reprieve from their ordinary lives. As time went on, we learned more about some of the kids. Many were consistently beaten, often by their parents. One boy confided that he had even tried to kill his abusive father. While their physical scars were obvious, their emotional wounds revealed themselves through violence toward each other.

We found out that most of the kids usually ate one meal a day and that they loved eating three meals a day at camp. On the last day of camp, as I brought my lunch plate back to the kitchen, I noticed a little girl finishing her soup all alone. What caught my attention was the stack of bread next to her piled at least ten slices high. My heart dropped like a brick as I realized she was hoarding the bread because she didn't know when she'd get another meal.

I had an emotional breakdown. I understood that I would soon be heading home to my comfortable bed and fully-stocked refrigerator, while these kids would be returning to the streets or to an orphanage. Many of them would continue to suffer abuse and lack of food. Their future seemed extremely hopeless to me. I wondered why a God who is so loving and so caring would allow these kids to suffer.

Our Scripture reading today shows us that Moses was uncertain of his calling to help free the Israelites. Even though God Himself showed up in a burning bush, Moses still had the audacity to tell

God he didn't think he could do the job. There are many notable points in this passage.

- God said in verses seven and eight that He saw the misery of His people and was concerned about them.
- He wanted to rescue them from their situation.
- When Moses questioned God, He responded with a simple yet definitive answer, "I AM who I AM." God is God.

We may not understand why God does what He does, but it's not up to us to comprehend His plans. It is our responsibility to accept them and to trust Him. We will never fully understand the mind of God, but we have the beautiful promise that He will guide us through the difficult times in life because He cares about us.

Prayer: *Thank You for being the God who created the world and the God who cares about me. You have proven that You love me, and I trust in Your plans for my life. Amen.*

How do you relate to Moses in the story from Exodus 3?

Notes/Prayer Requests & Praises

_____

_____

_____

_____

_____

_____

_____

Date 34: Silent Steps

Scripture Reading: 1 Timothy 2:1-4

I enjoyed helping out at my kids' school when they were little, but as my kids grew older, their schools needed fewer volunteers. I missed being involved in their classrooms, so I asked the schools if I could assist in other areas. One way I got involved was serving as a volunteer test proctor. How could I turn down a job with such a prestigious name?

As I oversaw exams one day, I realized that there was a higher purpose to being a volunteer test proctor. (I really enjoy using that title!) I decided I could use the testing time to pray by name for each of the students in my assigned computer lab. As I walked around the room, I prayed for the children. I prayed that God would protect them, that they would have a good school year, and above all, that they would seek God and know Him on a personal level.

When the students finished their tests, I made a point of telling them that they had done a good job, and I complimented each of them on something he or she wore. One time it happened to be Crazy Hat Day, so it was pretty easy to start conversations! I basically tried to be a bright spot in each of their days.

Today's reading says, "I urge, then, first of all, that requests, prayers, intercession and thanksgiving be made for everyone ... God our Savior wants all men to be saved." Maybe you don't have a school setting available to you, but you could go around your office and pray for each coworker by name. At the checkout line, you could silently pray for the clerk. As you drive through your neighborhood, you could pray over one house a day and ask God to be present in that home.

There are many unique ways to pray for people. Silent steps in prayer can make a huge difference even if the person you're praying for is a stranger. Start today by finding someone you can bless through anonymous prayer. You may never know the outcome of that prayer, but you don't have to know the result for prayer to be effective. God's Word can be trusted when it says that He wants all men to be saved. Your intercession can make all the difference.

Prayer: *Lord, thank You for allowing me to help change the world through prayers. Please help me to take notice of the people around me who need prayer. I am thankful that You want all men to be saved and to come to a knowledge of the truth. I want to take the time to pray for others even if I've never met them and will never see them again. Thank You for the power of prayer! Amen.*

Choose a stranger today and bless that person with prayer.

Notes/Prayer Requests & Praises

_____

_____

_____

_____

_____

_____

_____

_____

_____

Date 35: Spuds and Studs

Scripture Reading: Ephesians 5

One year my husband Barry generously announced that he and his brother were going to cook Mother's Day dinner for our families. I thought I'd died and gone to heaven! I pictured my sister-in-law and me relaxing on the couch while our husbands slaved away in the kitchen. It was going to be a great day.

There was only one itsy-bitsy problem: our husbands didn't know how to cook. The only things I'd seen Barry make were frozen pizzas and grilled-cheese sandwiches. My fears were confirmed on Saturday night as my husband and brother-in-law prepared their grocery list. It was quite comical. The menu was grilled chicken and baked potatoes, and before the guys left, my sister-in-law asked if they knew where to find potatoes. "Yeah, we'll just go to the store and buy baked potatoes," answered my husband (who limits his baking to frozen pizzas).

By now we were getting suspicious, so we asked them how they planned to prepare these baked potatoes. "We're going to grill them," replied my brother-in-law. We weren't too sure about that answer, so we asked Barry if he knew how to cook a baked potato. He seemed very sure of himself as he answered, "You chop them up and cook them in a pot." Hilarious laughter ensued when we asked them what part of baked potato they weren't understanding. When Barry asked if he should peel the potatoes before he boiled them, I was laughing so hard I almost lost it.

I'm not a fortune teller, but I could see a trip to McDonald's in our future. In the end, we didn't make a fast-food run and our meal was great. Barry cleaned the potatoes, and my sister-in-law wrapped them in foil and baked them. Our husbands grilled the chicken to perfection.

Recounting the events of that weekend, the words of Ephesians 5:25 come to mind. The verse says, "Husbands, love your wives, just as Christ loved the church and gave himself up for her." My husband showed he loved me by making an effort to do something that was out of his comfort zone. The man who makes only pizza and grilled-cheese sandwiches did his best to give me a special Mother's Day dinner.

When I close my eyes, I can still picture the beautifully set table. I can still taste the tangy flavor of the lemon-pepper chicken. I can still hear the unmistakable laughter of family. The memories of that Mother's Day will last forever, thanks to our husbands, the studs who dared to cook spuds!

Prayer: *Dear God, I want to follow Your example and love others even if that means doing something that doesn't come easily for me. I know that Christ loved me and gave Himself for me, and I want to serve others. I want my life to be a fragrant offering to You. Amen.*

Do something nice for someone this week, but to stretch yourself, do something that is out of your comfort zone!

Notes/Prayer Requests & Praises

_____

_____

_____

_____

_____

_____

_____

Week 6

Date 36: Loaded Questions

Scripture Reading: Proverbs 29

Have you ever asked someone, "How does this outfit look on me?" Now that's a loaded question! When I'm shopping, I want someone to give me an honest answer about how a piece of clothing looks on me. I'm serious! While I'd love to have a friend tell me it looks great, I want her to be truthful. I don't want to go home with clothes I'll never wear.

It's important that we have friends who will speak truthfully to us—not just about clothes, but about the important stuff, the hard stuff, the messy stuff. Friends who tell us what we want to hear might be good for our egos, but they won't help us grow.

"To flatter friends is to lay a trap at their feet" (Proverbs 29:5 NLT).

I don't like hearing that there are things in my life that must change. It's hard for me to acknowledge that I could have more patience with my kids or more grace with my husband. I don't like confessing that areas of my life require work, but I know I need to listen when a friend is trying to give me advice to help me grow into the person God wants me to be.

"To one who listens, valid criticism is like a gold earring or other gold jewelry" (Proverbs 25:12 NLT).

Valid criticism comes from a true friend who loves God and has your best interests at heart. Real friends want you to grow and maybe to change something in your life because they know that God is still working on you. I've learned a lot through the constructive criticism of people who have proven their friendship over time and who have earned my trust.

An important part of letting God refine you is being open to the help and advice of others. Like everyone, you see things mainly from your own point of view, and a trusted friend can offer valuable suggestions from a different perspective. Your job is to be open to receive that advice when it comes from a loving source.

"In the end, people appreciate honest criticism far more than flattery" (Proverbs 28:23 NLT).

Talking with a close friend, I shared some personal struggles. She listened quietly, then asked, "So what are you going to *do* about it?" This simple inquiry showed that she loved me enough not to let me whine and wallow. She called me to action, and in doing so, she gently refined me. I'm grateful she cared enough to ask that loaded question!

Prayer: *Heavenly Father, thank You for placing friends in my life who love me enough to ask the tough questions. May my heart be open to listen to them. I love You and want to continue to grow into the person You created me to be. Amen.*

How do you respond when someone asks you a loaded question? Is the Holy Spirit convicting you to have a heart-to-heart talk with a friend?

Notes/Prayer Requests & Praises

_____

_____

_____

_____

_____

Date 37: Miss Dee Meaner

Scripture Reading: Galatians 5:1-15

One year when my daughter Shalyn dressed up for trick or treating, she chose an interesting costume. Her shirt had pink-and-black horizontal stripes, and her pants were solid black. A chain with her supposed prison number hung around her neck. A pair of pink handcuffs dangled from her wrists as if they had been sawed apart right before her prison break. She labeled her costume "Miss Dee Meaner."

Ironically, around the time my daughter was choosing a costume, I was experiencing bondage in my life. I felt like I was in jail, but not the cute pink-bubble-gum jail from which my daughter supposedly escaped. My bondage came from multiple struggles that were bringing me down. With each new burden, I could almost feel the black metal bars of a jail cell closing behind me. I felt like a captive who was helpless to break free.

I tried to take matters into my own hands, but worrying only made me sick. I watched television and tried to forget my problems, but soon I realized that I was allowing trash to cloud my mind. I lay awake at night to pray, but instead of giving my problems to God and letting Him take over, I clung to them like a favorite blanket and tried to find solutions myself.

Then one morning I finally wrote down all of the problems that were holding me prisoner. I sat in silence and gave them to the Lord. Then I opened my devotional Bible and read Galatians 5:1-15 NLT, which happened to be my Scripture reading for the day. God is so good! The verses about freedom in Christ absolutely applied to my situation!

In verse 13, Paul says, "For you have been called to live in freedom, brothers and sisters." When I read those words, I felt as if the prison guard had taken the key to my jail cell, unlocked the door, and opened it wide. I discovered that I wasn't meant to live in bondage. In fact, this bondage was something I had chosen. It was self-imposed. By taking matters into my own hands, I had deliberately walked into that jail cell, sat down, and allowed the door to be shut.

The only difference between my jail cell and a real one was that I held the keys to the door all along. While convicts cannot get out of jail whenever they please, I had the choice to open my door at any time. The keys were sitting right next to me, but I chose not to use them. Every time I looked to myself to solve my problems, I snuggled a little deeper into the cell.

That day I realized that Christ did not die on the cross so that I would stay in bondage. He died so that I could live my life in victorious freedom. In fact, Paul said we've been called to live in freedom. Today I feel a little like Miss Dee Meaner. My chains are broken and I'm free!

Prayer: *Dear Jesus, thank You for calling me to freedom through the cross. When my sinful nature wants to overtake my faith in You, please remind me that You've given me the keys to freedom. Amen.*

Make a list of the problems and the stresses in your life. Now give them to God so that you can live in the freedom that is yours for the taking!

Notes/Prayer Requests & Praises

_____

_____

_____

_____

_____

Date 38: All I Need

Scripture Reading: Psalm 23

A dream I had one night is still vividly etched in my memory. It felt so real that when I woke up I wasn't sure if it was a delusion or a reality. In the dream, someone I loved was drowning. All of the people in the dream were in panicked desperation as they helped me search. No matter what we did to find this person underwater, we could not reach him. We experienced a horrible, helpless feeling as we searched for this loved one to no avail.

When I woke up, I still felt panicky. I wondered why I had experienced such a terrible nightmare. Then I realized that the dream was a metaphor for how I was feeling about my life. I felt overcome and desperate. Life was so overly busy that I could not seem to keep my head above water. I felt like I was going through the motions, surviving hour to hour.

As I thought back over the previous weeks and their multiple events, I wondered how I'd made it through that time. Of course the reason I was still sane was that God's strength was carrying me through each day. While I fully knew that God could and would continue to guide me, I also knew that the next few weeks would be just as full as the earlier ones. It was overwhelming.

That day my kids' devotional guided them to Psalm 23. It's such a popular psalm, and I almost didn't read it because of that fact. However, something prompted me to grab the closest Bible in our home and open it to this passage. I happened to grab the NLT Bible, and as I read the first verse I realized why this version was the one I "happened" to grab.

It read, "The Lord is my shepherd; I have all that I need."

Amen; let us pray. This verse is so powerful that I could meditate on it for days. This compact line says it all!

I read the remainder of the psalm, but that first poignant verse stuck in my mind throughout the day. With the Lord as my Shepherd, the Guide of my life, I had everything I could possibly need to get through the day, the week, and the month. This verse showed me that when I relinquish control to Him, I can trust Him to guide my life in every single detail. He can even take care of the details that will have to be worked out to get me through tomorrow. I don't have to panic, I don't have to worry; I can trust that He is all I need.

Prayer: *Lord, I want You to be the shepherd of my life. I realize that means I have to trust You more and to let go of the control I hold over my life. I can rest in the fact that in You I have all I need! You are all I need to get through this hour, this day, this week, this month, and this year. I am putting my faith in You, the Good Shepherd. Amen.*

Question: **What holds you back from allowing the Good Shepherd to be in charge of your life?**

Notes/Prayer Requests & Praises

_____

_____

_____

_____

_____

_____

_____

Date 39: Who Do I Think I Am?

Scripture Reading: Romans 14:1-8

Many years ago I was in a Bible study with a group of women. When we shared prayer requests after the study, I asked for prayer about a personal issue. "Please pray for me because I struggle with judging other people," I said.

I might as well have said, "Please pray for me because I'm a serial ax murderer."

The room fell silent and suddenly I realized that the subject of judging others must be taboo in the Christian world. However, I will address this battle of mine because you may struggle with the same problem.

If we take a good look at ourselves, all of us would probably have to admit that we have been guilty of judging others. I've been on both ends of judgment. I've judged others, and I've been judged. Neither spot is a good place to be.

In Romans 14:1-8, Paul makes it clear that as Christians, we are not to judge other Christians about disputable matters. I believe Paul is talking about matters that don't involve violating God's laws or are not black and white in Scripture.

Though Christians are supposed to be filled with the same grace extended by God through Jesus, we are often the first to judge. If we are convicted about something, we can easily fall into the trap of thinking that everyone around us should be convicted about that same thing.

In this Romans passage, Paul cuts to the chase about judging others. He says, "Who are you to judge someone else's servant? To his own master he stands or falls. And he will stand, for the Lord is able to make him stand" (Romans 14:4).

To rephrase this verse in my words, "Who do you think you are that you should judge other people? Only God can judge. Hold your tongue and let the Holy Spirit do His work."

When we are tempted to judge someone about a disputable matter, we need to take a big step back. By judging another, we are saying that we know God's will for this person's life better than the Holy Spirit does. Is that a place we want to be? When I feel the temptation to judge someone else, I ask myself, *Who do I think I am?*

Prayer: *Lord, please forgive me for all of the time I've wasted judging others. Holy Spirit, please convict me when I start to judge someone else, and remind me that You are the judge! I don't want to cause dissension in the church body. I want to encourage others and not judge them. Thank You for the example You set of grace through Your Son Jesus. I want to extend grace to others just as You extended grace to me! Amen.*

Do you agree that it's hard to admit to judging others? If so, why do you think that is?

Notes/Prayer Requests & Praises

_____

_____

_____

_____

_____

_____

_____

Date 40: Father Knows Best

Scripture Reading: Exodus 18:1-27

When my husband and I were first married, we had our eyes on a car we wanted to purchase. We had both recently graduated from college and money was tight. Hoping for advice about our situation, we decided to call my parents and run the idea by them. All we heard on the other end of the phone line was silence—a silence that spoke volumes! We knew they were not in favor of our impending purchase. In the end, we decided not to buy the car.

Exodus 18 recounts a story about Moses seeking advice. The chapter title in my Bible reads, "Jethro Visits Moses." My initial thought was, is this *The Beverly Hillbillies*? You don't see a name like Jethro in the Bible very often! That show was way before my time, but I remember that Jethro was a character in the series. Jethro is also the name of Moses' father-in-law.

Jethro (the one from the Bible) played an important role in Moses' life. He helped take care of his daughter and grandsons while Moses was away. When they reunited, he listened to Moses as he shared what God was doing in his life. Then Jethro rejoiced with Moses and they praised God together.

As Jethro spent time with Moses, he saw how much Moses was working. Moses was serving as judge for the Israelites, who required his attention from morning until evening. Moses was overworked! Jethro noticed this and told Moses that if he continued at this pace, he'd wear himself out. He told Moses, "Listen to me and I will give you some advice, and may God be with you." Jethro then suggested ways to divide the work among other capable leaders.

Thank goodness for family and close friends who can see areas in our lives that must change and who care enough to talk to us about them. It didn't hurt that Jethro had tangibly shown Moses he cared about him by building a relationship with him. Verse 24 says, "Moses listened to his father-in-law and did everything he said."

The moral of this story is that sometimes people who are older and wiser than we are can help us make good decisions. They've been around the block a few more times than we have! We can learn valuable lessons from their mistakes and their successes.

Wise old Jethro also gave me the opportunity to talk to my kids about why they should listen to their parents, their teachers, their pastors, and other sensible adults. It was a valuable lesson I was all too eager to share!

Father Knows Best is another TV show from before my time that fits with what I'm trying to say. With that show in mind, I would like to suggest a new title for Exodus 18: "Father-in-Law Knows Best." Jethro, you've got the leading role!

Prayer: *Dear God, may I not be too prideful to turn to others for advice. Just as Moses took advice from someone more experienced than he was, I want to gain wisdom from others who have been in my shoes. Thank You for giving us the body of Christ so that we can support each other. Amen.*

Think of a time when you have needed advice and have approached someone for help. Take time today to thank that person by phone, e-mail, or a written note.

Notes/Prayer Requests & Praises

_____

_____

_____

_____

_____

_____

Date 41: What Do You Expect?

Scripture Readings: Matthew 7:1-5; Romans 15:7-13

One day I was venting to my husband about frustrations with a friend. After listening patiently, he told me something I'll never forget. He said, "Gretchyn, you expect too much out of people."

I couldn't believe he had the nerve to say that to me! It was a comment I didn't want to hear because it was painfully true. I am definitely guilty of putting unrealistic expectations on my friends, my family, and especially my husband.

Some expectations are fine. I expect my kids to work hard in school, do their chores at home, and show respect to others. However, I can't expect them to be perfect. They are going to fight with each other. They are going to fail. They are going to do things that make me want to crawl into a hole. I cannot have unrealistic expectations for them, and I need to love them even when they let me down.

When Barry and I were first married, I had lofty expectations of him. I wanted him to have a good job, treat me like a queen, be frugal with money, and spend all of his free time with me. That wasn't asking too much of my brand-new husband, now was it? Basically, I wanted him to give me the world on a silver platter, and when that didn't happen, I was disappointed.

I had raised my expectations of him to such a high level that there was no way he could reach them. It caused a lot of tension in our marriage when he wanted to golf on Saturdays rather than spend time with me. I didn't realize that since he excelled at golf, playing eighteen holes was a way for him to do something he was good at and to blow off steam—steam produced in part by the weight of my expectations!

The book *One Month to Live* contains a powerful section about accepting others. Authors Kerry and Chris Shook suggest that we should stop trying to change the people around us and not only accept them, but try to understand them. Romans 15:7 guides in this area as it states, "Accept one another, then, just as Christ accepted you, in order to bring praise to God."

Virtues like honesty, trust, and loyalty are essential to relationships, but other things are not. If we're looking to others to meet needs that only God can meet, our expectations will always fall short.

Prayer: *Lord, I want to look at others through Your eyes. I don't want to judge others or put unrealistic expectations on them. Just as You accept me as I am, please help me to accept others. I want to bring You praise by accepting others as Your beautiful creations. Amen.*

What do you expect out of people? Think of one person whom you need to accept as is so that you can bring praise to God, then treat that person accordingly this week.

Notes/Prayer Requests & Praises

_____

_____

_____

_____

_____

_____

_____

_____

Date 42: My Pea-Size Brain

Scripture Readings: Judges 14:1-3, 15:3-8, 16:1-30

Sometimes I wonder, *How could God ever use someone like me to glorify Him?* It's a mystery why He would want me with all of my faults and my insecurities. As I read the Old Testament, though, I see many examples of how God used imperfect people to accomplish His perfect will.

Take the story of Samson. I don't get it! This man was supposed to be a judge for Israel, yet his life left a lot to be desired.

For starters, he definitely had a weakness for the wrong women. Samson was attracted to a Philistine (a member of a tribe that oppressed the Israelites for forty years). Samson was determined to wed this woman and told his father, "I want to marry her. Get her for me." In other words, I want what I want, and I want it now!

In a strange turn of events soon after they were married, Samson left his wife and returned to live with his father and his mother. Later, when he decided he wanted his wife back, he discovered she was given in marriage to the best man at his wedding. Acting out of anger, Samson tied torches on the tails of three hundred foxes and set them loose to burn down grain fields that belonged to the Philistines.

The Philistines came after Samson, looking for revenge. Scripture says the Spirit of the Lord came upon Samson and he used the jawbone of a donkey to kill a thousand Philistines. Instead of praising God, however, Samson boasted about his heroics and spent a night in the town of Gaza with a prostitute.

As I read about these events in Judges, my finite mind tries to reconcile the fact that Samson is a judge and a womanizer. He's a Nazirite (he took a vow to be set apart for God's service) who's filled with rage and anger. My mind struggles to comprehend how God can use such a sinful man for His purposes.

The beginning of the end for Samson came when he fell in love with a woman named Delilah. I guess you could say that she was the death of him. But even in that death, God used Samson for His purposes.

My pea-size brain tries to understand the mind of God, and I come up short. No surprise there! But through the life of Samson, I see that God can use anyone He pleases to accomplish His purposes. Even me—despite my shortcomings.

Prayer: *God, Your ways are not my ways, and Your thoughts are not my thoughts. I acknowledge that You have plans to use me for Your glory despite my faults. Please take my failures and my weak areas and use them for Your glory. I am humbled that You love me and have a purpose for my life. Amen.*

What faults or insecurities are holding you back from serving God?

Notes/Prayer Requests & Praises

_____

_____

_____

_____

_____

_____

_____

_____

Week 7

Date 43: Fast-Food Gods

Scripture Reading: Exodus 32:1-29

Life in America is definitely lived at a fast pace. If you don't believe me, just read some of the names of the businesses in my area: Quick Clean Car Wash, Quick Mart, Quick Fix Massage Shop, Kwik Trip (a gas station), Express Window Cleaning, Express Employment Professionals, Express Care, Fast Signs.

Do I want to experience a quick massage or express care? Is an express employment professional someone I want to hire?

I perpetuate this constant drive for quick results in my daily life. I get frustrated when my computer can't run five programs at once. When I encounter drivers doing only the speed limit, I look for an opportunity to pass them. At the grocery store, I always scan the aisles, looking for the shortest line.

I was surprised to see that the children of Israel also acted impatiently. While Moses was receiving the Ten Commandments, the Israelites decided they didn't want to wait for him. Exodus 32:1 says that when the people saw how long it was taking Moses to return from the mountain, they complained to Aaron, saying, "Make us some gods who can lead us. We don't know what happened to this fellow Moses, who brought us here from the land of Egypt."

Allow me to paraphrase: "We are tired of waiting. We want fast-food gods and we want them now. We don't care if the one true God has led us out of slavery and is taking us to the Promised Land. If God won't do what we want right now, we can't be bothered to wait. Make us some false gods."

We have to be careful that we don't expect God to produce results for us with the speed that we anticipate at McDonald's or the instant cash machine. God is not our express teller. God will answer us according to His timing, and His timing is always best! God wants us to be faithful to Him in prayer and patient in waiting for Him to answer.

We cannot have a fast-food mentality when it comes to a relationship with God. We can't develop a deep and lasting relationship with the Lord if we don't spend quality time with Him. We can't expect a premium steak at Burger King. There's no such thing as a fast-food God.

Prayer: *Oh, God, I know that You want to have a relationship with me. You sent Your Son Jesus to take on my sins so that I can know You personally. Please forgive me for taking You for granted. Forgive me for wanting a deep relationship with You but not putting in the time to read Your Word to get to know You better. I don't want to know You in a "fast food" way. I want to wait patiently and listen for You to speak to me. Amen.*

In what ways do you try to rush your relationship with God?

Notes/Prayer Requests & Praises

_____

_____

_____

_____

_____

_____

_____

Date 44: The Nerve of Some People!

Scripture Reading: Genesis 24:1-27

I can't believe the nerve of some people—telling God what to do. That takes guts, audacity, and stupidity all rolled into one!

Abraham's servant had the nerve to tell God what to do. It all started when Abraham told his oldest servant, the man in charge of his whole household, to find his son Isaac a wife. That was a tall order! The servant hesitantly agreed (as if he had a choice!) and traveled to Abraham's homeland to find his master's son a wife.

Can you imagine what was going through the servant's mind as he made this journey? *Why did Abraham choose me for this task? Isn't this a little above and beyond my job description? Why didn't I put in for early retirement?* It's easy to see why this servant may have been a little stressed out when he reached his destination. As he sat by a well outside of town, he laid out a plan that he wanted God to follow. It was pretty comical.

He said, "O Lord ... See, I am standing beside this spring, and the daughters of the townspeople are coming out to draw water. May it be that when I say to a girl, 'Please let down your jar that I may have a drink,' and she says, 'Drink, and I'll water your camels too,' let her be the one you have chosen for your servant Isaac" (Genesis 24:12-14). Laying out a specific plan for God took a lot of nerve!

Before the servant had finished praying, a young woman named Rebekah came out with her water jar and filled it. The servant asked her for some water from her jar. She replied, "Drink, my lord ... I'll draw water for your camels, too" (Genesis 24:18-19).

Bingo! Ding, ding, ding ... we have a winner! However, the servant wasn't so sure. The passage says he watched her in silence, wondering whether the Lord had made his journey successful.

Really? Let me get this straight: the servant laid out a specific plan for God, watched God answer his prayer to the letter, then wondered if this woman was the right one? My first reaction after reading this passage was, *Duh! Of course she's the one!*

Then I thought about how many times God has answered my prayers and I have failed to realize it at first. How many times have I forgotten to thank Him when He has answered me? Of all the nerve! In the end, the servant gave praise to God, bowed down, and worshiped Him. I don't want to have the same nerve as Abraham's servant. I want to seek God's plan for my life, then give Him the glory for answered prayer.

Prayer: *Dear Father, thank You for all of the times You've answered my prayers. You work in my life so often, and I want to notice all of the great ways You provide for me every day. Thank You for what You've done in my life today and this week. Amen.*

Right now I want to thank God for _____. (Feel free to make the list as long as you like!)

Notes/Prayer Requests & Praises

_____

_____

_____

_____

_____

_____

Date 45: J-O-Y Spells Prayer

Scripture Reading: Psalm 18:1-3, 16-19

After reading that title, you may think I'm a little crazy! Yes, I do know how to spell the word *prayer*, so please don't go searching for my grade-school teachers to let them know what a bad speller I am. I truly believe that prayer is spelled J-O-Y.

Have you ever noticed that your prayer life is becoming monotonous? At our house, we catch ourselves saying the same prayers over and over. Most of the time we say, "Thank you for this food" or "Thank you for this day" or "Thank you for dying on the cross for our sins." None of these prayers are wrong, but when we pray the same words all the time, those words can start to mean less to us.

You've probably heard the saying "Jesus, Others, You spells J-O-Y." It means that putting Jesus first, others second, and yourself last will result in a joyous life. It's a good concept to adopt in life. It also works with prayer. I decided to try it with my two kids.

I told them that we were going to change our prayers to include Jesus first (thanking and praising Him for one of His many attributes), others second (praying for someone else), and then you (praying for a request about themselves). After I explained this method, I looked into two sets of eyes staring blankly back at me. The kids seemed underwhelmed by my new prayer method.

I could see this new concept might take a while to sink in. When we started praying with the JOY method, the most challenging part was calling to mind God's attributes. Thank goodness for the book of Psalms! We found many words we could use to praise God—He's merciful, He's righteous, He's our Creator, He's our Protector, just to name a few!

Changing the way our family prays has helped us to focus our attention on God and to learn more about His attributes at the same time. We have discovered that His characteristics are limitless! Now, without using a dictionary or thinking about what you learned in school, how do you spell *prayer*?

Prayer: *God, so many of Your qualities go unnoticed unless I search for them in Your Word. Please forgive me for the times when I am stagnant in my prayer life. I want to give You the praise and honor You deserve, and I want to do it creatively. Thank You for the many facets of Your being. You are such an amazing God! Amen.*

Read today's Scripture passages one more time. Write down all of the attributes listed for God. Then take a moment to praise Him for those attributes.

Notes/Prayer Requests & Praises

_____

_____

_____

_____

_____

_____

_____

_____

_____

_____

Date 46: Bright Red Lights

Scripture Reading: 1 John 1

Driving on snowy and icy roads is something everyone from Minnesota must learn, and one night my winter driving skills were put to the test.

It was snowing and windy, a treacherous combination. Hesitantly, I pulled out onto a two-lane highway behind a semitruck. I was reluctant to follow the semi because I thought it would be going too slowly. However, just the opposite happened. The semi sped along on the icy roads. Since visibility was poor, my only hope was to follow the truck's bright red taillights.

Ironically, the same truck that had frustrated me a few minutes earlier was now providing light to guide my way home.

As I struggled to keep up, I thought about those lights as a metaphor for my relationship with God. As I follow Him, I often feel that He is going too fast for me to keep up. I am reminded that during those times, I need to focus on the Light and follow close to Him.

Finally, I turned off onto a county road. I was relieved that I could now drive at a comfortable speed. I settled in for a more relaxing drive home, but my relaxation was short-lived.

Soon I saw red flashing lights in the distance. As I got closer, I realized that these lights belonged to a snowplow—a very slow-moving snowplow! At this point, I wanted to get home as quickly as possible, and this lethargic vehicle annoyed me.

Then a smile came to my face as I once again realized the irony of my situation. First I had been forced to follow bright red lights that were going too fast. Now I had to follow bright red lights that were going too slowly. God sure does have a sense of humor, and He was definitely trying to drive home (pun intended) a point to me that night!

I need to follow God's light. Sometimes He takes me down roads more quickly than I would like. Other times He takes me on paths that seem painfully slow. Either way, I need to follow His light and seek His will. I need to trust that His lighted path is the right one for me.

Prayer: *Lord, sometimes it's scary to follow You. You choose to take me down roads more rapidly than I would like. Or sometimes You lead me down a road slowly, and in my impatience, I want to jump ahead of Your will. Please help me to be content traveling through life at Your speed. I realize that everything You do is for a reason. You have great plans for me, and I don't want to miss those plans! I acknowledge that following You means traveling at the speed You have set for me, and I am willing to travel at Your pace! Amen.*

Where are you in life right now? Are you behind a snowplow or a semi? Is God taking you down His path too quickly, or are you moving at what seems to be a snail's pace? No matter what speed you are traveling at right now, set your mind on seeking God's will for your life. Spend time with Him so that you can learn to be content with the speed of your life.

Notes/Prayer Requests & Praises

_____

_____

_____

_____

_____

_____

Date 47: Paul's Life Rules

Scripture Reading: 1 Thessalonians 5:12-22

I'll hazard a guess that you've heard of the Ten Commandments. Even if you can't recite all ten, I'm sure you could list quite a few. In the Old Testament book of Exodus, God gave the Israelites the Ten Commandments so they would know how to live holy lives. In the New Testament book of 1 Thessalonians, Paul gave believers some great rules for life. As I read today's Scripture passage, I was amazed at the relevance of his two-thousand-year-old instructions.

Please don't get mad at me, but I'm going to give you a little extra work today. I promise it will be worth it! **Read today's verses and write down every instruction you find. There are a lot of them. Use a separate piece of paper or the space provided in your book.**

How many instructions did you find? I found seventeen. I know it took extra time to write them all down, but aren't you glad you did? I was more than a little convicted by some of these guidelines, but I was also encouraged that I have been successful in observing a few of them. I want to expand on three instructions that God spoke about to me.

Paul says, "Honor those who are your leaders in the Lord's work" (1 Thessalonians 5:12 NLT). I hate to admit this, but sometimes I find myself being unnecessarily critical of Christian leaders. I needed to hear Paul's gentle reminder that they are only human, just like the rest of us. I should spend less time complaining and more time praying for them and encouraging them to do God's work.

Paul instructs us, "Take tender care of those who are weak" (1 Thessalonians 5:14 NLT). What struck me about this verse was the word *tender*, which can also mean loving, caring, affectionate, gentle, and compassionate. One of my dear friends has done a great job living out this instruction. While her husband fought ALS for many years, she affectionately stood by him and lovingly met his needs. As his primary caregiver, the tender way she loved him will be forever etched in my mind.

Another of Paul's instructions is to "Encourage those who are timid" (1 Thessalonians 5:14). Just the other day a friend reminded me of a time when I was coordinating a Mothers of Preschoolers group and she was a mentor mom. She remembered that I had asked her to give a devotional for the moms, but that she didn't think she could. She recalled, "You were kind of forceful when you told me that I could do it and that you would plan on me for the next meeting." We shared a good laugh about it. "In the end, I was glad you made me give the devotional because you forced me out of my comfort zone," she said. I didn't even know it at the time, but I guess I was following one of Paul's life rules.

Prayer: *Dear Father, thank You for giving me practical instructions for how You want me to live my daily life. I want to follow You, and I am thankful for Paul's specific instructions. Amen.*

Take the list of instructions you wrote from today's passage and pray over this list. Ask God to point out where you are doing well and where you need His help.

Notes/Prayer Requests & Praises

_____

_____

_____

_____

_____

_____

Date 48: My Mentor(s)

Scripture Readings: Ecclesiastes 4:9-10, 12; Proverbs 11:30, 13:20

It's funny how you think you know everything when you're young. At least that's how it was for me. As I grew older, I watched people in my life become more intelligent. For example, my parents weren't very smart when I was in high school, but when I went to college they got a lot more intelligent.

I have to wonder, did they really get smarter, or did I finally realize that I didn't know everything? I'm pretty sure I know the answer to that question!

No matter how it happened, the need for wise people in my life became evident. I desired a mentor to guide me along life's path. I longed for someone to take me by the hand, invest in me, and challenge me to be a better person. Unfortunately, finding a mentor was easier said than done.

I've tried not to take it personally, but I have never found a mentor. I've prayed long and hard about it. I've even begged God for one. Once I took a big leap of faith and asked someone to be my mentor, but the arrangement didn't work out.

Before you feel too badly for me or wonder what on earth could be so wrong with me that no one would mentor me, let me share how God provided for this need in my life.

Instead of giving me that one mentor I prayed for, God gave me multiple mentors. There may not be one specific person devoted to me, but God has blessed me with many people who guide me and encourage me. I can think of friends who inspire me, teach me, share Godly wisdom with me, listen to me, and give me sound advice.

In my ignorance, I asked God for one specific mentor, but He chose to answer my request more abundantly than I could have imagined. I am so thankful that God knows me better than I know myself. He is so much smarter than I am!

Prayer: *Heavenly Father, I am thankful that You have placed wise people in my life to guide me. You know me better than I know myself, and I trust You to give me what I need and who I need in my life! I thank You for the people in my life who mentor me. Please continue to direct me to wise mentors who are seeking You. Amen.*

Who has been a mentor to you? Write that person a thank-you note right away. Is there anyone you could mentor? Take time to pray about God's direction for you as a mentor.

Notes/Prayer Requests & Praises

_____

_____

_____

_____

_____

_____

_____

_____

_____

Date 49: Where's the Rest?

Scripture Reading: Exodus 20:1-21

The weeks can get busy around our house. I'm sure most people can relate to that. Activities, meetings, work, and the responsibilities of everyday life seem to take up any potential spare time.

One year our family was looking forward to a long Memorial Day weekend with a bonus day to relax. Although I would classify the weekend as extremely fun, it was not necessarily relaxing. While we enjoyed spending time with our extended family and working on home improvement projects, we were exhausted at the end of the weekend.

When I was reading my devotions the next week, I realized why I was so tired from the previous weekend: I didn't take time to rest. In Exodus 20, God told the Israelites that they should work for six days and on the seventh they should rest. God set the example when He created the world in six days and rested on the seventh day.

God knew what He was doing when He created us. He didn't create our bodies to go, go, go and never take a break. He created us to work hard, then take time away from work to regain our strength and focus on Him. I can see now that I wasn't following God's plan for my week. Sometimes we may even need to schedule rest during the week.

I made the right choice about my time in one instance. A Sunday on the calendar had started to fill up for me. The schedule for that day included church in the morning followed by a lunch meeting. Then I had about an hour before another meeting. When someone called and invited me out to dinner that night, I stopped to look at my calendar. My heart said yes to the invitation while my head said, *Are you insane?* Thankfully, I followed my head because by 6:00 p.m. that Sunday I was ready to be home!

If we don't dedicate time to the Lord and give our bodies a break during the week, God might ask us, "Where's the rest?"

Prayer: *Dear God, when You created the world, You set the example of how to work hard and of how to rest. You want me to dedicate time out of each week to spend with You. I want to follow Your example and give my body time to relax and to recuperate from the workweek. Please forgive me for the times when I haven't followed this plan and have overextended myself. Thank You for setting the example of how my week should look. Amen.*

Do you get enough time in the week for your body to rest? If not, what can you do to change that?

Notes/Prayer Requests & Praises

_____

_____

_____

_____

_____

_____

_____

_____

_____

_____

Week 8

Date 50: Cool Car Conversation

Scripture Readings: Deuteronomy 7:7-9; Exodus 35:20-22

Car trips can be a great opportunity for unexpected in-depth conversations. This was the case for my son, Caleb, and me one day when he had recently finished fifth grade. For the first half of our two-hour ride, I listened to him talk about things like basketball and his iPod. Then I apprehensively decided to broach the touchy subject of homeschooling.

As soon as I mentioned the topic, the car became uncomfortably quiet. The reason for the silence was that my husband and I had recently decided to homeschool our two kids, and Caleb was not at all happy about it. I had been dreading this conversation. After a few moments of silence, he asked, "Why do I have to homeschool?"

I told Caleb that his dad and I had never planned on homeschooling, but that God had worked in our hearts to bring us to this decision. As we prayed about it, we felt certain God was telling us this was the right choice for our family.

He asked, "How do you know when God is talking to you, because I've never actually heard Him?" Again there was silence, and now the ball was in my court. I thought back to the situations that led us to choose homeschooling. I believed that God had ordained each one.

"Well," I began slowly, "First God opened our hearts to homeschooling through your sister's interest in it. Then God put people in our lives who made us think about the benefits of homeschooling. God also used His Word to show us the importance of passing His laws to you and Shalyn. Every time I read the phrase *generation to generation* in the Bible, I felt God telling me that He wanted me to be the one to teach you two. That phrase kept popping up in my devotions, and I couldn't ignore the fact that God was speaking to me."

"What does it sound like when God speaks to you?" Caleb asked.

"Well, you know how your conscience tells you not to do something bad or to do something good? It's kind of like that when the Holy Spirit talks to you. He prompts you, sometimes quietly and sometimes loudly. When I brought all of my doubts about homeschooling you before Him, He quietly said to my heart, 'I've already told you what to do. Now please do it and trust Me.'"

Once again there was silence, but this time it was a thinking and a processing silence. I wanted to believe it was also an accepting silence, but I didn't know if Caleb was ready to let God change his heart about homeschooling quite yet. After all, God's timing is not always my timing! For the moment, I quietly thanked God for the cool car conversation with Caleb.

Prayer: *Lord, in Your Word You say You want willing hearts. May my heart be open to whatever You have planned for me. I love You and want to serve You. Please show me how to pass Your Word from generation to generation. Amen.*

How is God prompting you to pass His truths from generation to generation?

Notes/Prayer Requests & Praises

_____

_____

_____

_____

_____

Date 51: Don't Look at Me!

Scripture Readings: Daniel 4; Psalm 16:2

I read an interesting story one day in Daniel 4. King Nebuchadnezzar ("King Neb" for short) had a strange dream. He saw an enormous tree whose branches touched the sky. The tree was full of fruit and sheltered the beasts of the field and the birds of the air. King Neb saw a messenger from heaven who ordered the tree to be chopped down to its stump. The messenger said the stump should be drenched with dew and bound with iron and bronze. He then commanded that the tree's mind be changed from that of a man to that of an animal for seven years.

What a strange dream! Only Daniel knew what it meant, and he was certain King Neb didn't want to know the answer. After some deliberation, Daniel uttered the fateful words, "You, O king are that tree!" It must have taken courage and maybe a little stuttering to get those words out!

Daniel warned the king that unless he turned from his sins and acknowledged God, this dream would become a reality for him. One year later, the king was walking on the roof of his palace. If you can believe it, these are the words he spoke: "Is not this the great Babylon *I* have built as the royal residence, by *my* mighty power and for the glory of *my* majesty?" (Daniel 4:30, emphasis mine). Have you ever seen so many *I's* and *my's* in one sentence?

The words were barely out of his mouth when a voice from heaven announced that King Neb was stripped of his royal authority. He was driven out to the middle of nowhere and fed on grass like a cow. His body was drenched with dew, his hair grew like the feathers of an eagle, and his nails became like the claws of a bird. Grizzly Adams had nothing on him!

When the seven years were over, King Neb came to his senses and honored the Lord. He glorified and exalted the King of heaven. He realized that everything he possessed had come from God. The king admitted, "Those who walk in pride He is able to humble" (Daniel 4:37).

This story is a reminder that all good things come from God. If there is anything good in our lives, if we have any talents or skills, if we've been blessed in any way, we must give the glory to God. We should say, "Look at God; don't look at me!"

Prayer: *God, You alone give me what I need. Sometimes You give me more than I need, and I want to thank You for Your many blessings. I realize that You have given me everything good in my life and that all blessings are from You. I want to praise, exalt, and glorify You, the King of heaven, because everything You do is right and all Your ways are just. Amen.*

Take a moment to be alone with God and ask Him to show you any areas in your life that are prideful. Then ask Him to forgive you and to grant you humility in these areas.

Notes/Prayer Requests & Praises

_____

_____

_____

_____

_____

_____

_____

Date 52: Bless This Meal (Please!)

Scripture Reading: Psalm 92

Sometimes I offer to host Thanksgiving dinner. I use the word *sometimes* because cooking isn't exactly one of my talents. I often feel inadequate in the area of hospitality. A friend once came to my house and prepared Thanksgiving dinner for a large group of my in-laws. Another year, when I attempted the cooking myself, I forgot the potatoes. Thank goodness for stores that stay open on Thanksgiving Day! In other years, I've ordered an entire meal prepared by a local grocery store. All I had to do was heat it up.

No matter how the meal makes its way to the table, Thanksgiving is a time to reflect on the many blessings in our lives. One year when it was my turn to host, I thanked God for what turned out to be quite a unique list. I gave thanks for

- Sam's Club's premade mashed potatoes and stuffing;
- plastic bags to self-baste the turkey;
- those little packets that help make gravy;
- my mother-in-law, who made the pumpkin pies;
- the gift of a Wii that kept the kids entertained in the basement;
- my dear friend who helped me make my grocery list;
- a double oven (which I needed to deep clean from frozen-pizza spillovers);
- my health, so that I could make the attempt at Thanksgiving dinner; and
- family members and the grace they needed to eat the dinner set before them.

I am about as far away from Martha Stewart or Rachael Ray as anyone can get. However, I am happy to say that almost all of the food on the table that day was edible!

In all seriousness, I have a lot to be thankful for. I live in a country where I can vote for my government leaders. I can worship God without persecution. I have food to eat and a great home. I have a wonderful family and amazing friends. My inability to cook seems to pale in comparison with the many blessings God has given me!

Prayer: *It is good to praise You and to make music to Your name, O Most High, to proclaim Your love in the morning and Your faithfulness at night. I will sing for joy at the works of Your hands. How great are Your works, O Lord, how profound Your thoughts! Thank You for the many blessings in my life. Amen.* (From Psalm 92)

What are three blessings in your life? Write them down and take a moment right now to thank God for them.

Notes/Prayer Requests & Praises

_____

_____

_____

_____

_____

_____

_____

_____

_____

Date 53: The Dilemma

Scripture Reading: 1 Corinthians 10

One day when I was reading my Bible I realized I had a dilemma. The funny thing was that I didn't even realize I had one until I read my devotions for the day.

I'll quote the verses and then I'll explain the dilemma. Paul says, "Everything is *permissible*, but not everything is *beneficial*. Everything is *permissible*, but not everything is *constructive*. Nobody should seek his own good, but the good of others" (1 Corinthians 10:23-24, emphasis mine).

Later in the chapter, Paul says, "Do not cause anyone to stumble ... for I am not seeking my own good but the good of many, so that they may be saved" (1 Corinthians 10:32-33).

As I read those verses, I realized I would face a situation at an office Christmas party later that evening in which I could do something permissible, but not necessarily beneficial or constructive. I could do something permissible and possibly cause someone else to stumble, or I could abstain with a clear conscience.

As I read the verses, it occurred to me that God placed them in front of me on a day when I would have to make a choice. It just happened that I was reading 1 Corinthians 10 that day, but this was no coincidence for God. He ordained and scheduled those verses even before I knew I needed them.

The more I thought about this passage, the more I realized it could be a valuable filter in so many areas of our lives. Just as a furnace filter stops junk from getting into our home or a dryer filter catches the lint from our clean clothes, this verse could be a filter for decisions in our lives.

We could think of this verse before we overeat, before we choose a movie, before we speak, or before we make a financial decision. We could use this verse as a filter for almost anything in our lives.

When I make coffee, I use a filter to keep the unwanted grounds out of my delightful hot drink. I also drink filtered water from my fridge. If I'm taking precautions to filter what goes into my body, I should also filter what's going into my mind.

Prayer: *Lord, I know I have a choice as to what I put in my mind. Please help me to use 1 Corinthians 10:23 as a filter for decisions I make. I want to make choices that glorify You. Please give me the strength to choose the things that are beneficial and constructive according to Your will. Please open my heart and my mind and show me the gray areas I need to change. Amen.*

Write out 1 Corinthians 10:23 and tape it to your fridge, your phone, your TV, your checkbook, or any other area of temptation. Use it as a filter for your mind. It will be interesting to see what seeps through this filter—and what doesn't!

Notes/Prayer Requests & Praises

_____

_____

_____

_____

_____

_____

_____

Date 54: Don't Skip a Step

Scripture Reading: Deuteronomy 11:18-25

This is a little embarrassing to admit, but sometimes I try to run up the stairs in our house and I miss a step. You can imagine what happens next. I trip and fall in the most awkward way. The lesson is, I need to watch where I'm going so I don't miss a step.

It's the same with our Christian walk. There are steps to follow. If we miss one, we might find ourselves sprawled out on the stairs, so to speak! Following steps is important in every field. For example, would you want someone who had completed a CPR class to perform heart surgery on you? Probably not! You'd want that person to go through years of proper medical training before you felt comfortable about letting him crack open your chest.

Deuteronomy 11:18-20 spells out the steps we should take as followers of Christ. First we must study the Bible and get to know God in a personal way. We need to carve out time for Him in our daily lives through Scripture reading and prayer. Verse 18 says, "Fix these words of mine in your hearts and minds; tie them as symbols on your hands and bind them on your foreheads." Isn't that a great image of the importance of committing God's Word to memory?

The next step is to teach what we've learned to our children, bringing our spiritual knowledge into family life. Verse 19 says, "Teach [these words] to your children, talking about them when you sit at home and when you walk along the road, when you lie down and when you get up." That's pretty much all of the time! We should put God's Word into practice throughout the day.

When we have established a habit of studying God's Word and are bringing it to family members, then we are ready to go into the world. Verse 20 says, "Write [Scripture] on the doorframes of your houses and your gates." God wants us to take what He's taught us into our communities and throughout the world.

Sometimes in our Christian walk it's tempting to run too fast and skip a step. Take it from me, it's no fun to lie on the stairs in pain. It's far wiser to take the Christian life one step at a time.

Prayer: *Heavenly Father, thank You for sending Your Son Jesus to die on the cross so that I might have a personal relationship with You. I want to get to know You better by searching Your Word daily. Please give me knowledge and insight to share in my home with my family members so that they may also grow in You. When I am ready, please show me how I can reach my community and the world for You. I love you! Amen.*

What step have you reached in your spiritual journey? Where would you like to be?

If you're looking for a verse to memorize, start with Psalm 119:105: "Your Word is a lamp to my feet and a light for my path."

Notes/Prayer Requests & Praises

_____

_____

_____

_____

_____

_____

_____

Date 55: Praying and Playing Drums

Scripture Reading: Psalm 33

What a difference a day makes! I had heard this saying before, but during one memorable weekend I realized just how true it was—although I think it should be changed to "What a difference a day of prayer makes!" Allow me to explain.

I was scheduled to play drums for the worship team at church one Sunday. Our team had practiced on Thursday night, and to say that I didn't play well would be an understatement. I had messed up too many times to count. By the time Saturday rolled around, I'd let my self-deprecating thoughts convince me that I'd ruin worship and make a fool of myself in the process. I was terrified! I needed God more than ever, so I sat down to ask Him for help. Here is an entry from my prayer journal on that Saturday.

"Lord, I want to glorify You on the drums tomorrow. I need You to take my meager ability and multiply it! I can only do this through Your strength. I am claiming Philippians 4:13 NLT, 'I can do everything through Christ, who gives me strength.'"

Writing that prayer helped calm my fears and get me through the day. There was precious little time to practice on Saturday, so I needed to trust God for musical ability that could come only from Him. On Sunday morning I read Psalm 33, then I wrote another prayer in my journal.

"Lord, Psalm 33 says to 'Sing joyfully to the Lord ... Praise the Lord with the harp [I inserted the drums], make music to Him on the ten-stringed lyre [again, drums], sing to Him a new song, play skillfully, and shout for joy.' Lord, I really need You! Please guide my hands and feet so that I may play skillfully. I will give You all the honor and glory."

The only way I was going to play skillfully was if God took over! There was absolutely no way anyone was going to shout for joy if I played like I had in practice. I had to depend on God to take my drumsticks and to use them for His glory. He answered my prayer in a huge way! Here's my journal entry from Sunday night.

"Lord, thank You for being my hands and feet today. I could feel Your presence throughout the service. Thank You for answering my prayers. You showed Yourself through the music, communion, and pastor's message. You are an amazing and awesome God!"

Sometimes I try to live my life in my own strength and I don't rely on God. Then when things start going wrong, I wonder why my life is a mess. Playing the drums undoubtedly stretched my faith. On my own, I couldn't make a joyful noise, but God made a joyful noise through me. I'd prefer to have my life planned out and scheduled so that there are no surprises or unknowns. However, the Lord knows that I need experiences like playing the drums so I'll depend on Him.

Prayer: *Father, I admit that I need You in every area of my life. There is not one thing I can handle with my own strength. Thank You for always standing right beside me! Amen.*

What areas of your life do you need to give to God? Hand over the drumsticks!

Notes/Prayer Requests & Praises

_____

_____

_____

_____

_____

Date 56: Where I Fit

Scripture Reading: Acts 6:1-7

Have you ever given your time to something that didn't fit your talents? For instance, I've come to realize that I am not gifted at working with young kids. I've been there, done that, and barely lived to tell about it. Truth to tell, it wasn't that bad, but working with those precious little ones definitely wasn't within my comfort zone.

I was a Mothers of Preschoolers coordinator for many years. Serving with this organization was a perfect fit for my personality and a great use of my abilities. I loved helping moms with young children get the support they needed, and I enjoyed managing the leaders who assisted these moms. I was able to use my leadership and organizational skills along with the gift of my just-crazy-enough-to-be-sane personality.

In a perfect church, all members would have the luxury of serving in positions that used their gifts. However, we know there is no such thing as a perfect church in our imperfect world. Even the early church, which is a great model for us today, struggled in this area. Today's Scripture passage recounts a difficult situation that the church encountered.

Some of the Jews felt that their widows were overlooked in the daily distribution of food, and they came to Paul for a solution. He must have felt this wasn't his area of expertise, because he wisely explained that his focus had to be on "prayer and the ministry of the word" (Acts 6:4). Instead of personally taking on the matter of feeding the widows, he delegated the job to others so that he could serve where he was proficient.

My husband once attended a conference on how to be a more effective leader. He learned that, in business, it's wise to focus on cultivating people's strengths instead of trying to improve their weaknesses. He discovered that people are happier and more productive when they use their strengths versus spending time in areas where they struggle.

I'm not suggesting that you serve only in areas where you are gifted. There is definite value in serving outside of your comfort zone. One benefit is that you might learn something new. Another benefit is that you will come to appreciate other people and their gifts. For instance, I now have a deep respect for people who work with little kids! Yet another benefit is acknowledging the deep need to trust God for the abilities that you lack.

God created you with a unique skill set, and He did it so that you could honor Him. Just like Paul, you need to find what gifts you have and confidently use them to do God's will. I love the freedom that comes from discovering where I fit into God's plan.

Prayer: *Dear Father, thank You for creating me and for designing me with a special purpose in mind. I want to do my best to fulfill that purpose. I humbly ask You to show me how I can use the unique talents You've given me to best serve others. Amen.*

Where do you fit? If you're unclear about your gifts, there are many Christian books available to help guide you. Check out a Christian bookstore or an online Christian book retailer.

Notes/Prayer Requests & Praises

_____

_____

_____

_____

_____

_____

Week 9

Date 57: Good Gifts

Scripture Reading: 1 Corinthians 13

Valentine's Day. Some people think it's a big scheme by Hallmark and floral shops to swindle money out of the public. Others believe it's the perfect time to show a loved one how much they care about him or her. I enjoy using Valentine's Day to remind family members that they are special to me. After all, it's the only day of the year when my son asks for pink pancakes, when I can give my daughter a cute stuffed animal, and when I get to send my husband to work with a large bag of red licorice to share. (At least that's what he is supposed to do with it!)

On February 14, kids usually take candy to pass out at school to show their friends they care about them. Adults give flowers, gifts, or cards as a way of expressing love and affection.

It was fitting when our family's morning devotions one Valentine's Day included John 3:16, "For God so loved the world that He gave His one and only Son, that whoever believes in Him shall not perish but have eternal life." Reading this well-known verse on this popular day made me realize that the day God sent Jesus into the world is the true Valentine's Day!

However, it doesn't have to be Valentine's Day for God to express His love for us. He shows us He loves us every day of the year. "How great is the love the Father has lavished on us, that we should be called children of God! And that is what we are!" (1 John 3:1). God loves us, which is not just a good gift but an awesome gift!

In Matthew 22:37-39, Jesus talked about loving God and the people in our lives. He said, "'Love the Lord your God with all your heart and with all your soul and with all your mind.' This is the first and greatest commandment. And the second is like it: 'Love your neighbor as yourself.'"

Reciprocate the love the Lord has shown you by spending time in His Word and in prayer today. Then make a special effort to show love for someone around you. It can be a family member, a cashier at the gas station, a neighbor, or anyone else you encounter throughout the day. You don't have to wait for a holiday loaded with candy and Cupid's arrows to give good gifts!

Prayer: *Dear Lord, thank You for Your unconditional love for me. While I was still a sinner, You sent Your Son Jesus Christ to die for me. I want to follow Your greatest commandment, which is to love You with all of my heart, my soul, and my mind. Please show me through Your Holy Spirit how I can love You completely. I also want to love my neighbors as myself. Please open my eyes to the needs of hurting people in my life so that I may show them Your love in tangible ways. I love You! Amen.*

Give a good gift to someone in your life today. Write a note or send an e-mail to say what you appreciate about this person.

Notes/Prayer Requests & Praises

_____

_____

_____

_____

_____

_____

_____

Date 58: Just Wing It

Scripture Reading: Acts 3:1-20

Do you know someone who enjoys speaking in front of people? I know a few brave souls who like public speaking, but why they like it is beyond me! I'm much more comfortable behind a computer.

My husband's job often requires him to speak at seminars. It never ceases to amaze me when, on the night before he's scheduled to speak, he offhandedly comments, "I suppose I should think about what I'm going to say tomorrow." I think to myself, *Did he really just say that? Does he honestly not have every last word planned out yet?*

Maybe I have trouble relating to his spontaneity because when I speak to a group, I plan way ahead. I have whatever I'm going to say written out at least a week before I speak whether I'm addressing fourth- and fifth- grade girls or a group of women. It scares me to death to think about just winging it!

In our Scripture reading today, Peter and John heal a crippled beggar. Soon a crowd gathers around the two disciples, who have drawn attention because of the miracle they performed. I adore verse 12, which says, "Peter saw his opportunity and addressed the crowd" (NLT). God presented Peter with a group of avid listeners, and Peter seized the moment! I'm so impressed by him! God opened the door for Peter to explain who gave him the power to heal the lame man, and Peter wasn't afraid to wing it. He didn't have an eloquent speech prepared, but God worked through him anyway.

The second year I coached girls' seventh- and eighth-grade tennis, God gave me an opportunity to wing it. On the first day of practice, I visited my doctor, who diagnosed me with a chronic pain condition. My doctor advised me to minimize stress, get plenty of rest, and exercise every day for ten minutes at a time.

I chuckled to myself because I knew I was entering a season when I'd be exercising two hours a day, and the doctor's advice seemed comical.

As the season came to a close, the pain intensified. The final two weeks of the season brought extreme fatigue and discomfort. I know I made it through that time only because God's strength sustained me during each hour of each day. At our end-of-the-year party, God prompted me to share this story with the girls. I concluded by telling them that God would be there for them no matter what they faced in their lives. I didn't have a planned speech and I was sweating like crazy, but God gave me the words to say. He gave me what I needed to wing it!

Prayer: *Lord, You know how difficult it can be for me to speak in public. However, I know that when You give me the opportunity to share Your message with others, You will be faithful to give me the words to say. Thank You in advance for Your faithfulness and for giving me confidence to declare the message of Your love to others. Amen.*

What do you need to do to be ready when God wants you to wing it?

Notes/Prayer Requests & Praises

_____

_____

_____

_____

_____

_____

Date 59: How Do You Give?

Scripture Reading: 2 Chronicles 31:1-13

What comes to mind when you hear the saying "God loves a cheerful giver"? My wacky mind pictures a cartoon of a man with a sheepish smile holding an offering plate. Maybe that's because I read too many Sunday comics as a child. No matter what you picture when you hear that adage, the truth is that giving doesn't always come easily. Depending on your financial circumstances or how you were raised, it can be a struggle to give with a cheerful heart.

A friend told me that she gets frustrated because it seems that her church is constantly asking for money. I've heard people say that as soon as they make more money, they'll start tithing. Still others have told me that they grew up feeling that they had to give out of guilt and duty, and they can't seem to break away from the past.

In 2 Chronicles 31, we read how King Hezekiah dedicated himself to showing the people of Judah how to be cheerful givers. We can learn a lot about giving as we look at specific ways the people gave to the Lord.

They gave out of their first share. I love this because it shows that they didn't wait until they could afford to give; they gave immediately out of the first part of their harvest. They gave the first share of their grain, new wine, olive oil, honey, and produce. One of my friends writes out his tithe check before paying any of his other bills, which is like the people of Judah giving their first share.

They gave generously. The fact that they gave generously has huge significance because it shows they gave cheerfully, not grudgingly. When we give generously, we most likely give more than is required. Verse 5 says, "They brought a large quantity" (NLT).

They gave faithfully. Verse 12 says, "The people faithfully brought all the tithes and gifts to the Temple" (NLT). It doesn't say they brought their tithes when they felt like it or when they had extra olive oil or honey. They gave faithfully, which means consistently. Giving faithfully requires that we trust that God will meet our needs.

When King Hezekiah saw the huge piles of food and donations, he asked the priests and the Levites where all these gifts had come from. The high priest replied, "Since the people began bringing their gifts to the Lord's Temple, we have had enough to eat and plenty to spare. The Lord has blessed his people, and all this is left over" (2 Chronicles 31:10 NLT). How do you give to the Lord?

Prayer: *Lord, I want to give generously. I want You to have control over my finances. Please show me what I need to do so that I can give generously and faithfully out of my first share. Show me specifically what that means in my life. I want to honor You in all areas of my life out of a cheerful heart. I love You and want to serve You wholeheartedly. Amen.*

Which one of the three ways of giving listed above do you struggle with and why? Pray about it and ask God to help you overcome this difficulty.

Notes/Prayer Requests & Praises

_____

_____

_____

_____

_____

_____

Date 60: Divine Assignments

Scripture Reading: Proverbs 3:5-6

One morning the kids and I were reading a devotion about "divine assignments." (I'm not talking about the 007 type of missions, but pretty close!) There are many examples of divine assignments in the Bible. Mary's was to give birth to the Messiah. It's hard to top that one! Moses had the divine assignment of freeing the Israelites from slavery. These were clearly tasks ordained by God.

The kids and I started thinking about how we could be involved with God's divine assignments. What would these look like for a stay-at-home mom and two grade-school-age kids?

The kids had some great ideas, such as helping someone at school who was hurting or including a classmate who often got left out. My ideas were to encourage a friend or to write a blog entry that could draw someone closer to Christ. We prayed that God would show us His divine assignment for that day, and then the kids left for school.

I didn't have long to wait for mine to be revealed. Soon after the kids left, a friend called. She had been going through a rough time, and immediately I knew my divine assignment was to encourage her. The Scripture passages I'd been reading fit in perfectly with the issues she was dealing with, so I shared what the Lord had shown me.

Fortunately, I was ready for my divine assignment and had the tools to help my friend. There have been times when I was not in the Word and would not have been able to help someone in need. I was thankful that I'd been reading the Bible and that God could use what He'd been showing me to help her.

Another friend is often presented with divine assignments at her workplace. Coworkers and even clients come to her for advice and for wisdom because they know her knowledge comes from the Lord. Some of her divine assignments are unexpected and take time out of her busy day, but I know that the Lord uses her daily to encourage those around her.

We all have divine assignments. We just have to look for them and perform them when they arise. If you don't feel that you have any divine assignments, pray that God will give you one. Just make sure you're reading the Word daily so you have the tools to complete the assignment!

Prayer: *Heavenly Father, I want You to give me divine assignments. I know I need to be in Your Word and in prayer so that I will see the assignments when You present them. I want to be ready and waiting when an assignment arises, and I want to be used by You. Amen.*

Write down the names of people who have been on your mind lately. Pray that God will show you a divine assignment for one of these people.

Notes/Prayer Requests & Praises

_____

_____

_____

_____

_____

_____

_____

Date 61: Hard to Share

Scripture Readings: 1 Timothy 6:6-10; Mark 10:17-31

Minnesota is called the Land of 10,000 Lakes and we have the license plates to prove it! Some people (Minnesotans, of course) say that ten thousand is a conservative estimate. No matter what the number might be, that's a lot of lakes! One year my husband and I were thrilled to be able to buy a small cabin on a lake—our little weekend retreat.

I had a lot of plans for that cabin. Snapshots of family togetherness scrolled through my mind like a slide show. I dreamed about all the special times the four of us would spend boating, playing games, or sitting around the campfire and roasting marshmallows. I envisioned peace, serenity, and most of all, solitude. My husband, however, had a different dream for the cabin. As we drove home after finalizing the purchase, he began listing all the people he planned to invite to the cabin.

Since I'm somewhat of an introvert, you can imagine what happened to my anxiety level when his dream and my plans did not align. The more I thought about his dream the more I panicked. A very different slide show permeated my thoughts. I envisioned myself cooking, cleaning, hosting, entertaining, and then getting groceries so I could cook some more. His dream of sharing our cabin was invading my dream of privacy and family time!

In Mark 10:17-31, Jesus told a rich young man to sell everything he had, give the money to the poor, then follow Him. The Bible says the man's face fell and he went away sad because he had great wealth. He didn't want to share his possessions.

How does this relate to our cabin? The Lord blessed us with the cabin. But instead of wanting to use it to bless others, I wanted to keep it for myself. According to 1 Timothy 6:10, the love of money is the root of all kinds of evil. It wasn't wrong to have a cabin, but it was wrong to love it so much that I wasn't willing to share it. We eventually decided that we would divide summer weekends at the cabin evenly, half for our family alone and half for time with guests.

If I have any possession that I can't bear to lose, I probably shouldn't own it. If I obtain a possession that I'm not willing to share, I probably shouldn't have that either—whether it's a car, a television, a cabin, or a home.

Prayer: *Jesus, I know You expect me to put You first in my life. Please show me if there are any material possessions that I could not bear to lose. I want to put You ahead of anything I own. I do not want to love money more than You. Please show me anything that is hindering me from loving You or reaching out to others. Amen.*

Think about your valued possessions. If God asked you to share one of these possessions, would you? If the answer is no, pray about it. Ask God to help you give Him, not the possession, the place of honor in your life. Warning: you might need to get rid of the possession!

Notes/Prayer Requests & Praises

_____

_____

_____

_____

_____

_____

_____

Date 62: Boomerang

Scripture Readings: Psalms 74, 75

You're probably familiar with the flying tool known as the boomerang. You might be picturing it in your mind, since its V shape is quite distinctive. The most common type is called a returning boomerang. It's designed to travel on an elliptical path and to return directly to its point of origin.

The boomerang can accurately represent periods in our relationship with God. Some of my friends are in the midst of hard-hitting trials. Maybe you are experiencing an extremely difficult situation, or maybe you're praying someone through a tough time. You might feel like crying or even screaming out to God.

The writer of Psalm 74 did just that. Asaph (or possibly one of his descendants) was obviously frustrated as he boldly shared his feelings with God. He said, "Why have you rejected us forever, O God?" (Psalm 74:1). Can you believe He asked God that question? Don't hold back, Asaph! Tell us how you really feel!

In my early twenties, I was in a Bible study about prayer. The book we used taught us that we can lay it all on the line with God— even our rawest emotions—because He can take it. This doesn't give us the right to be disrespectful or to doubt God's plan for our lives. However, it means we can come openly to God and share our deepest fears, desires, frustrations, and heartaches. The God who created us can handle our emotions.

We can cast our burdens on God, but just as the boomerang always returns to its original point, we must return to praising God in the midst of our circumstances. We can cast our cares on Him and then resume our praise.

In Psalm 75:1, 9, Asaph says, "We give thanks to you, O God, we give thanks, for Your Name is near; men tell of Your wonderful deeds ... As for me, I will declare this forever; I will sing praise to the God of Jacob."

Prayer: *Lord, I want to be honest with You about my feelings, realizing that You have the best plan in mind for my life. I don't know why bad things happen, but I know that You can work all things together for good. During hard times, I will trust in You. Amen.*

What can you praise God for today? Make a list.

Notes/Prayer Requests & Praises

_____

_____

_____

_____

_____

_____

_____

_____

_____

_____

_____

_____

Date 63: Sacrificial Jewel

Scripture Reading: Luke 21:1-4

One Mother's Day sticks out in my mind. For a special treat, my family had taken me out for lunch and then to shop. I used the day to my advantage—I even dragged the three of them into a home store with me. (You can imagine how much my husband and my son enjoyed that!) As I was browsing, my husband and my young daughter mysteriously disappeared. I found out what the secrecy was about a little later when my daughter proudly presented me with a pink-jeweled dangly-butterfly decoration.

It wasn't the gift itself that I loved as much as the fact that she spent her own money to buy it for me. This little jeweled butterfly still hangs above my computer, and I will always remember that it was purchased out of love.

Our final stop that day was Target. My daughter said she had $16 and some change to spend, so we stood in the toy aisle while she made her selections. She chose three small toys and we headed to check out. The cashier said her total was $16.34, but as she counted her money, she found she had only $13. To my surprise, she quickly chose one of the toys and gave it back to the clerk.

On the way home, I thought more about our trip to Target, and it dawned on me why my daughter didn't have enough money to buy all of the toys. It was because she had spent some of her money on me! Suddenly the gift's value increased exponentially because I realized she had to sacrifice a new toy to give me the butterfly.

I was reminded of the widow's offering in Luke 21. This woman was very poor, yet she gave everything she had to God. She gave out of her poverty, the truest form of sacrificial giving. When the widow gave all of her money to God, she chose to live by faith and trusted that God would meet her daily needs.

We can give in many ways. We can bless someone financially, but we can also bless others with our time and talents. God wants each of us to listen to the Holy Spirit's prompting when we see needs around us.

This story brought a thought-provoking question to mind. Am I giving out of my excess or am I giving out of my poverty? When I set aside myself and my needs and my wants to help others, I am giving sacrificially. God wants every part of our lives, not just the surplus. He wants us to give until we have to trust Him to meet our needs.

Prayer: *Dear Savior, even though the widow in Luke gave only a small amount of money, You said that she gave more than those who were wealthy. I want to surrender to Your will and give out of a heart of sacrifice, not out of surplus. Thank You for giving me the example of this widow. Please show me where I can give to my family, my community, and my world. Amen.*

How is God prompting you to give your time, money, or possessions? Brainstorm some specific ideas.

Notes/Prayer Requests & Praises

_____

_____

_____

_____

_____

_____

Week 10

Date 64: Eighty-Five Sheets

Scripture Reading: Matthew 5:13-16

When I was a child I loved to read. That love for reading turned into a love for writing, which turned into a bachelor's degree in journalism. Years after being a stay-at-home mom, a friend invited me to a writing conference. The conference prompted me to write a blog, which is now a book. However, I would never have gotten to the book part if not for the prodding of a dear friend.

On my fortieth birthday, another friend presented me with a special gift: a printed copy of my blog entries—all eighty-five of them! Yet it wasn't just the paper and the ink that made the gift so touching. It was the meaning behind the gift.

We all need people to believe in us when we don't have the courage to believe in ourselves. My friend saw the potential that my blog held. She knew it had been a big part of my life, and she also realized that it was sitting unfinished and abandoned. So with that stack of paper, she gave me something much more valuable than a pile of printed words.

She gave me hope. She gave me strength. She gave me the courage to believe in myself and the gift of writing God had placed in my heart as a child. By handing me those eighty-five sheets of paper, she in essence said, "You are valuable and what you have to say is valuable."

If not for that friend's encouragement, this book would probably not be in print and you would not be reading it right now. The book itself holds no value, but the truths written in it are full of life and light because they are from God's Word.

I would have hidden that light under a bushel and stayed in my comfortable little world, but my friend knew that I needed to step out of my box. I will always be grateful for her immeasurable kindness. While there is no way I can ever repay her, I know she would want me to pay it forward by encouraging others to use their abilities. God has blessed all of us with unique gifts and talents. Sometimes it just takes a little push from a friend to give us the courage to use them.

Prayer: *Heavenly Father, You are the giver of good things. You have blessed me with unique talents and gifts. How do You want me to use them? How do You want me to encourage others to use their gifts to honor You? Please open my eyes to notice the talents of those around me and give me the insight to speak up and inspire them to serve You in a powerful way. Amen.*

Find one person this week to encourage in a special ability he or she possesses.

Notes/Prayer Requests & Praises

_____

_____

_____

_____

_____

_____

_____

_____

Date 65: Not-So-Green Thumb

Scripture Reading: Psalm 92

The other day I drove by the flower mart in town, and I just had to stop. This is unusual for me because I do not have a green thumb. I'll admit it was the 50 percent off sign that drew me in. My mom, my sister, and my aunts maintain beautiful greenery, but somehow I missed out on that gene. Once someone gave me a vine and told me vines were virtually impossible to kill. Well, I did it. I killed a vine!

Despite my not-so-green thumb, there is one plant I have come to love: the hosta. Hostas are so hearty that even I can't kill them. Over the years, I have learned how to divide them, and each spring I transplant them to another area of my yard or give them away. However, I wasn't expecting these plants to provide me with a good laugh.

One day when I was dividing the hostas, I called a few people to ask if they wanted my spare plants. No one accepted my offer, so I had my son take the extras to the backyard and I forgot all about them. A couple of weeks later, a friend came over and complimented me on the hostas in my front yard. She's an avid gardener, so I was proud of myself as I told her how I divided them up each spring and usually had some left over.

She asked me what I had done with the extra plants, and I told her they were in the backyard. She wanted to look for them, and we found that my son had placed them on some cement blocks behind my shed. She asked if she could take them and plant them at her home. To my surprise, those forgotten transplanted hostas soon flourished in her yard!

There's a verse in Scripture that mentions transplanting. Psalm 92:12-13 NLT says, "But the godly will flourish like palm trees and grow strong like the cedars of Lebanon. For they are transplanted to the Lord's own house. They flourish in the courts of our God."

Just as those hostas survived and even thrived in their new home, someday we will not only live but flourish in heaven. I love the verses that say the Godly will be transplanted into the Lord's house. Oh, how I want to be uprooted and replanted at the home of the Master Gardener! My hope lies in the fact that because I know Jesus, someday I will live with God and will flourish in His courts. Maybe in heaven I will finally have a green thumb!

Prayer: *God, thank You for the hope of heaven. Thank You that I can live with that hope if I accept Your Son Jesus as my Savior. Thank You for the promise of eternal life with You. I can't wait to be transplanted someday from this sinful earth to the glorious home You're preparing in heaven for those who love and serve You. Amen.*

What do you most look forward to about heaven?

Notes/Prayer Requests & Praises

———————————————————————

———————————————————————

———————————————————————

———————————————————————

———————————————————————

———————————————————————

———————————————————————

———————————————————————

Date 66: It's Soooo Easy!

Scripture reading: 1 John 3

One of my high school teachers used a phrase that still echoes in my head today. After he'd finish his lesson, he would say in a low, patronizing voice, "It's soooo easy." The tiny word *so* was never as long as when he would drag it out. That phrase always made me feel like an idiot if I didn't catch on to what he was teaching that day.

I was reminded of this phrase the other day when I was reading John's first epistle. I came across one simple verse that epitomizes the Christian life. "And this is His command: to believe in the name of His Son, Jesus Christ, and to love one another as He commanded us" (1 John 3:23). In that one verse, the essence of what it means to be a Christian is revealed. Living the Christian life isn't always easy, but God made it easy for us to understand what being a Christian is all about.

The first part of that verse says that we become children of God by believing in the name of His Son, Jesus Christ. John 6:40 says, "For my Father's will is that everyone who looks to the Son and believes in Him shall have eternal life, and I will raise them up at the last day." Believing in Jesus is not easy for some people. They will cite many reasons for not believing in Him. However, to those who choose to believe in Him and are willing to trust and to serve Him, He has promised eternal life.

The second part of the verse says we must love one another as He commanded us. This is where the proverbial rubber meets the road. This is where we show we are true disciples of Christ. After we accept Christ, we are instructed to love one another. Notice that there are no stipulations to this verse. (I kind of wish there were!) What about the coworker who has it in for us? What about the Christian friend who has hurt us? What about that family member who works on our last nerve? What about people who have done despicable things? Are we really supposed to love them?

The end of this verse makes it clear that we are called to love *everyone*. Sometimes it's not "soooo easy" to love certain people. It's easy for me to love people who are kind to me. It's a lot harder to love people who are difficult.

God set the ultimate example of love (see Romans 6:23) by sending His only Son to die for a sinful world. That sinful world includes you and me. We have done nothing to deserve God's love, yet while we were still sinners, Christ died for us.

Loving others can mean different things to different people. Some people love others by helping those in need. Some people show love by participating in mission trips. Some people show love by choosing to forgive those who have hurt them. Other people show love by reaching out to others in their communities. No matter how God wants you to show love, the important thing is that you do it.

Prayer: *Lord, I believe in the name of Your Son, Jesus Christ. I want to obey Your command by loving others. Please show me how to love others around me and in other parts of the world. Thank You for Your sacrifice of love for me when You sent Your Son to die on the cross for my sins. Amen.*

How is God asking you to love someone today?

Notes/Prayer Requests & Praises

_____

_____

_____

_____

_____

Contact Information

REDEMPTION
PRESS

To order additional copies of this book, please visit
www.redemption-press.com. This book is also available on
Amazon.com and BarnesandNoble.com,
or by calling toll free 1-844-2REDEEM.

For more inspirational readings or to contact
Gretchyn Quernemoen, please visit her
website at www.grace-for-today.net.

CPSIA information can be obtained
at www.ICGtesting.com
Printed in the USA
FSOW02n1427260117
30004FS